THE BUSINESS OF
Writing & Editing:

PRACTICAL TIPS & TEMPLATES
FOR NEW FREELANCERS

© 2015 Sagan Morrow

ISBN: 978-1-68222-659-9 Print

ISBN: 978-1-68222-660-5 eBook

TABLE OF CONTENTS

INTRODUCTION: HOW I GOT STARTED AS A FREELANCE WRITER & EDITOR

Starting at the Very Beginning

My story is, I think, a pretty typical one. Ever since I could hold a pen—before I even knew how to print letters—I would scribble on paper and pretend to write. Once I learned my letters, I started writing stories. I lost track of the amount of stories I wrote. Most of them were fantasy novels with thousands upon thousands of words, accompanied by maps illustrating the imaginary lands that I created and a dictionary of the words that I designed for my new languages.

Between the ages of eight and 18, I probably wrote somewhere in the range of 20+ novels.

It was around my late teens that I began to shift my focus from fiction to nonfiction. I started to become more interested in the world around me than the worlds that I created. I also became very interested in healthy living (specifically, nutrition and fitness). At this point I was doing a fair amount of reading online, and one blog that I loved was written by a health writer, Leslie Goldman. It had never occurred to me before that someone could be a *health writer*, but since I was so fascinated by health and I still loved to write, it seemed to be the perfect career option for me. I emailed Leslie inquiring how she got started, and she graciously agreed to a phone call Q & A.

Leslie was the person who advised me to start my own health blog. She explained that if I started out by blogging, it would give me practice as a reader, enable me to figure out if writing about health was really what I wanted to do, and also provide me with some writing samples to build up my portfolio. And so my first blog, Living Healthy in the Real World, was born.

I started out on Blogger, moved to Wordpress.com, and finally purchased my own domain name (www.livingintherealworld.net, which I switched to SaganMorrow.com in February 2015), using Wordpress.org as my platform. Over the years, I watched as my blog grew and grew. After my first year of blogging, I began to get requests from companies to do product reviews in exchange for free books, food, and even running shoes!

And in October 2009—less than two years since I had started my blog— POM Wonderful flew me down to California with 14 other bloggers on their first-ever Blogger Harvest Tour to tour the orchards on foot and by mini plane and to be wined and dined. I was the only Canadian blogger who had received the invitation, and it was the first time that it really hit home that I could make something of myself with this writing business.

Exploring My Passions and Interests

During this whole time, I was attending university. I had grown up with the understanding that university was just "what you did." My parents weren't concerned with what degree I got or with whether I would go on to graduate school; they just wanted me to get a degree in *something* to help me get farther in life. Since I liked learning, that made sense to me, and I happily went to university right after high school.

I started university assuming I'd get my degree in Psychology (I had always enjoyed my introductory psychology class in high school), but my professor was a bore in first-year university and besides, I found out that I would have to take a statistics course if I got a degree in Psychology. Frankly, I was tired of math (and clearly I didn't want to get into Psychology *that* badly), so I decided to get my degree in English instead, since I loved writing.

And then, after only barely starting to take some English courses, I discovered that our university had a Rhetoric, Writing, and Communications department.

I had never heard of such a department before but it sounded pretty fantastic to me. The subject material included everything from analyzing advertisements to interpreting fairy tales to talking about our understanding of gender as a society to learning about communication theories and more. It was basically an entire degree in critical thinking, and it was absolutely perfect for me.

While I was in university, around the time that I decided to switch to the Rhetoric department, I grew interested in the student newspaper—and thanks to my health blog, I soon became the newspaper's health columnist. I wrote a weekly column on health and wellness, recipes and nutrition, fun and easy fitness routines; the works. I even applied for a position as the Copy and Style Editor at the newspaper, but I didn't get it (probably because of my complete lack of qualifications at the time!).

Even though I didn't get the Copy and Style Editor position, the managing editor at the newspaper (who happened to be best friends with my sister) offered me another position that to this day I'm sure she invented on the spot: to proofread the entire newspaper before it went to print. It wasn't a paid position, and it had never been available as a volunteer position before, but I jumped in happily. Tuesday evenings became one of my favourite parts of the week, and I felt such a thrill every time I caught a typo, formatting error, or punctuation mistake which had been missed by the writer, section editor, and managing editor. I knew then that editing was for me.

In my last year of university, I also started another blog: Living Rhetorically in the Real World. I began writing about the things I was learning about in university and about communications in general. I was starting to get interested in writing about other things besides just health.

I completed my degree in Rhetoric, Writing, and Communications in 2010, writing my final exam the same week that I moved into my newly-purchased condo. I was a new homeowner, I had a degree under my belt, and I was ready to get out into the real world and start my career.

...Except that I didn't know what my career would be. I was stuck! What could a person do with a degree in Rhetoric, anyway?

My First Foray into Freelancing

I got lucky. If I'm honest, it was luck that played a major role in helping me along my way to becoming a freelance writer and editor. I knew that I wanted to edit, but I also knew that to get hired with a big publishing company, 99.9% of editors required a degree in Publishing. I didn't want to go that route—much as I loved learning, I was tired of the education system and wanted to finally have a "real job." So I sent my resume off to dozens of local publishing companies and advertising agencies and even a public relations company in the hope that someone would bite.

Meanwhile, a family friend, who was the past editor of our city's newspaper and who heard that I wanted to break into the writing and editing industry, passed my name onto a creative agency when they offered *her* a freelance gig that she was unable to do herself. That simple act of passing my name on led to a wonderful long-term relationship between me and the creative agency. Ever since that initial project, the company offered me more work a couple times each year for the next four or five years. They weren't always very big projects, but they were something!

Almost at the exact same time as I first met with the creative agency, the owner of a local public relations company (which I had sent my resume off to) reached out to me as well. As it happened, he had just signed a contract with a local health centre. Based on my background in health writing and my passion for health and wellness, he decided to take a chance on me—even though I had no knowledge of writing press releases or connecting with the media.

The rest of my opportunities grew from these two initial people taking a chance on me. I received a contract job as the communications person with a new non-profit (a fruit picking and sharing organization) and became a full-time freelance writer for about six months. But when my contract with that fruit sharing non-profit ended, I panicked!

I didn't think I could continue to find work, and I had this mortgage to pay too. At this time, it is also worth noting, I didn't do much research into *how* to succeed as a freelancer, and I was making some critical mistakes such as working in my pajamas at home (which we'll talk about later). So I applied for a job that paid $14 / hour (a big difference from my freelance gigs, most of which paid $40 or $50 / hour) at a local provincial registered charity. I got the job, and I stayed there for a full three and a half years while continuing to do part-time freelance work on the side.

My position at this registered charity shifted dramatically over the years. At one point I wore four different hats: I was the coordinator for a healthy food project, I was in charge of development and fundraising for the organization, I was the youth outreach coordinator, and I was also in charge of the wellness and fitness of the office staff.

In short, I was burned out, exhausted, and drastically underpaid, even with my $2 / hour raise. My boss was a lovely woman, but she and I didn't agree on a lot of the copy for our promotional and fundraising materials, and we had different ideas about how to go about doing things. It was time to leave, and I decided that now was also the time to make the big leap and become a full-time freelance writer and editor—again.

My Second, Successful Foray into Freelancing

After making the decision to become a full-time freelance writer and editor, I stayed for five months at the charity while I researched how to become a freelancer and start my own business, and planned where I would find work. I gave the charity four weeks' notice before starting out on my own in April 2014.

Thanks to my years of doing freelance work part-time (which I had continued to do in the evenings and on the weekends while I was working at the charity), I already had a few somewhat steady clients that I was working with when I started freelancing full-time. There was the real estate agent that I wrote monthly blog posts on downtown living for, the children's book author for whom I proofread books whenever she had new ones ready for publishing, and of course the creative agency which had technical documents to edit or poster copy to be written a couple times each year. In January 2014, I was also hired by our local university to transcribe class notes for deaf and hard-of-hearing students.

And that brings us to the first important lesson I want to share with you in this book: **start your full-time freelancing business when you already have relationships with at least a few clients.**

Contrary to one of the common freelancing commandments, I did not have six months' worth of income in my savings account when I left my 9–5 job. I only had perhaps two months' worth. While I certainly wouldn't recommend that anyone else jump into freelancing without much in the savings account, it also meant that I had to *really* hustle for work during those first few months—*and I think that was good for me.* It meant that I had to be successful immediately; there was no concept of, "oh, if this doesn't work, at least I can still live comfortably for a few months before I have to find a job!" No: instead I worked extremely hard to make sure that I could pay all of my bills, and it paid off.

I did plenty of research in the months leading up to April 2014—which is the second important lesson I would suggest if you are going to become a freelancer (and which you've already made a great start at by reading this book!).

I researched how to find work as a freelancer, how to structure my days, and what to do during the peaks and troughs of freelancing, but I was frustrated that I didn't just have *one* place I could go to for finding really great, practical, useful information. Mostly, I picked up tips and tricks here and there as I went along, simply through my own experience as a freelancer.

What This Book is All About

As a freelancer, you can learn a lot through personal experience. But is it always really *necessary*? What if you could pick up a book and have another person's successes and failures, their mistakes and learnings, their recommendations and tips and tricks and advice, all laid out for you at your fingertips?

That was the idea behind writing this book. I would have loved for a really great, comprehensive, easy-to-read resource to refer to as I made the switch from working a 9–5 job to becoming a full-time freelancer, and I hope that this book can be that for you.

My goal here is to make your life easier as you start your own business as a freelance writer / editor. Although this book is specifically for writers and editors starting their own freelance business, you should still be able to make good use of it if you are starting out as a freelancer, business owner, or entrepreneur in just about any field.

This book will provide you with recommendations for how to set your rates, tips for finding and maintaining clients, advice for managing both the busy and the slow times with your business, and so much more. Throughout the book, you're going to discover real-life examples and stories from my own experiences, incorporated with general advice and tips.

At the back of this book, you will also find some appendices with your very own editing checklists to make your life that much easier, a business plan template that you can make use of to start your own business, a sample of what a day in the life of a freelancer looks like to prepare you for your new lifestyle, and a few other fun and practical resources.

Welcome to the world of business, freelancer!

CHAPTER 1: THE FREELANCE LIFESTYLE (OR, WHAT DOES A WRITER / EDITOR DO?)

This is, of course, the big question! What the heck does a writer / editor do?

The answer to this question is a little complicated. Sure, a writer writes and an editor edits, but depending on the type of project, the amount of work needed, the medium that the document is in (for example, print vs. web), and what the client wants, your version of writing or editing may differ drastically from project to project and client to client.

But let's try to keep it simple:

What Does a Writer Do?

The difference between a high-quality writer and a poor-quality writer is immense. Poor-quality writing can mean fewer sales, reduced credibility as a business, and a poor reputation overall. But a *good* writer can reverse all of that! A high-quality writer can increase sales and enhance a business' credibility and reputation. This is what a good writer attends to and does:

- Researches and reviews their client's business, products or services, industry, and target audience to ensure a thorough understanding of who the client is, what the business does, and what the industry is all about, as well as who the target audience is and how best to engage those people.

- Creates, writes, and puts together relevant, engaging content for the business (this, of course, is the main thing people think of when hiring a writer!).

- Edits (and sometimes publishes, in the case of blogs, for example) the content they have written.

- Identifies and makes good use of relevant, appropriate, and engaging headlines, key words, and images.

- Advises and makes recommendations on promoting and marketing the content and using it as a tool for the business.

- Adapts writing style, tone, voice, format, and content based on the business, target audience, and medium.

- Ensures all writing is clear and concise and has been proofread.

What Does an Editor Do?

A professional editor looks at someone else's (or their own) writing, and can do the basics of proofreading to the more complex developmental and structural editing. Here's what an editor generally does when they are at work:

- Reviews for (and fixes!) typos, grammatical errors, and spelling mistakes.

- Compares the writing with relevant style guides and adheres to them.

- Checks for consistency in the content of the writing.

- Provides comments and recommendations on word choice, writing style and voice, and best practices for appealing to and engaging with readers.

- Formats the work where necessary to ensure it flows as smoothly as possible.

- Critiques and offers a reader's perspective on the material before it goes public.

- Rewrites vague or convoluted sections.

- Researches and fact-checks as needed.

- Identifies gaps or areas where more content is needed.

- Ensures that all work is publisher-ready.

As you can see, writing and editing can be quite different, although there is certainly a fair amount of overlap. In my experience, by engaging in both activities (writing and editing), you can actually become better at both of them. I would encourage anyone who is interested in either writing *or* editing to participate in the other on a periodic basis so as to enhance the skills of your main interest.

What about Specific Types of Writing and Editing— Such as for Blogs & Social Media?

This is a great question! Since I began freelancing full-time, I've done a fair amount of social media management. In December 2014, I attended the Elite Blog Academy to take my lifestyle blog, SaganMorrow.com, to the next level, and become a professional blogger as a key component of my freelancing business.

Many freelance writers will take up some type of social media work at some point in their career, especially in this day and age—so it's good to know what you're getting yourself into if you choose to do this type of writing.

These are some of the things that a social media manager and / or professional blogger does on a regular basis:

- Creates and edits content (as outlined above in the descriptions of what writers and editors do).
- Curates content (in other words, pulls together articles and images from other sources and credits them appropriately when sharing them).
- Prepares editorial calendars and schedules content or shares it live.
- Researches client industries.
- Researches and stays updated on the latest social media and blogging news and tips.
- Puts together and reviews strategies and plans.
- Analyzes, interprets, and evaluates analytics and adjusts strategies.

- Builds a following and engages with the community.

- Takes photos (or searches for photos on stock image sites) and edits images.

So now we've covered what a writer / editor actually does when they are at work, but what about the freelance lifestyle? In other words, how does a freelancer spend their days?

What the Freelance Lifestyle Looks Like

Life as a freelancer varies drastically depending on your personality and work ethic / style! Because you get to be your own boss, you also have the freedom to do your work when you are at your most productive. The flexibility of freelancing is extremely freeing—although it can also be daunting or overwhelming if you've never worked this way before.

Here are some of the things that worked well for me, when I first started freelancing full-time in 2014:

- **Waking up at approximately the same time each day and starting my weekdays with some exercise.** When I first began freelancing, this was so important to me for gathering the energy I needed and for keeping myself in good shape. It's good to have a simple routine first thing in the morning to set you up for success for the rest of the day.

- **Getting dressed before I started working.** This has made a huge difference for my productivity. I have a specific area of the house that is dedicated to my home office, and I dress just as though I were going to an actual office for the day. I'm not saying that everyone is going to be more productive by getting out of their pajamas—some people might work great in their pajamas—but for me, this is what works.

- **Starting my workday by going through emails and updating social media.** When I first started freelancing, sometimes this only took me 30 minutes; other times, it could take up to two hours. I get a lot of my work through social media (more on that later), so it is crucial to my business model that I maintain all of my social media platforms and update them daily. Nowadays, this activity can take me as little as 10 minutes.

- **Taking long breaks in the afternoon.** Usually I hit a "slump" in the early- to mid-afternoon. So when I first began full-time freelancing, I would take a break at that point until I felt eager to work again! Sometimes this meant I'd start working again at 6pm when my energy perked up.

- **Separating the weekends from the weekdays by wearing lounge clothes on the weekends.** The only days of the week that I wear pajamas or lounge clothes for much of the day (instead of actually getting dressed) are weekends or the occasional holidays. I often say that the only thing that separates my weekdays from my weekends is the types of clothes I wear—other than that, my weekdays and weekends blend together!

- **Working pretty much every day of the week.** The thing with being a freelancer is that you don't really get "sick days" or "vacation time." You have to save up for them! Because of that, I generally work seven days of the week.

However, I also pay close attention to my body. If I wake up one morning and am not feeling so hot or I feel a little sluggish, I'll only work a few hours and take the rest of the day off. This means that sometimes I'll go for several weeks without really taking a break, and other times I'll only work four days of the week for a few weeks. Listening to your body is extremely important.

More than a year later, here are a couple more things that have worked for me (with a few changes from the year before):

- **Exercising in the middle of the day instead of first thing in the morning.** This is one of the biggest changes I have made, which has had a really interesting impact on my day. I find it nice to wake up in the morning and have breakfast at my computer while quickly reviewing emails and social media, and then I can dive right into writing.

   It also means that exercising breaks up my day nicely: I can do one kind of work in the morning, then exercise, and then get started with a different project in the afternoon. Exercising in the middle of the day gets me out of the house (since I go to the gym for fitness classes), and it gives me an extra burst of energy right around the time that I'd normally hit my "slump."

- **Replacing long afternoon breaks with other kinds of work.** This includes my daily lunchtime workout as mentioned above, as well as often doing some cleaning around the house while I listen to a podcast or a webinar related to business, freelancing, blogging, etc.

   I like that this way of taking a break keeps me productive without burning me out: the trick is to get away from the computer and exercise a different part of your brain when you start to get tired with work. Then you can come back to your work feeling refreshed—and your house and workspace will be a whole lot cleaner, too.

There you have it! Those are some of the main things to know about my personal way of managing the freelance life. Other than that, it changes daily depending on the type and amount of work I have. It often feels as though clients are whispering together and agreeing to send things my way all at the same time, because I'll have a few days without any work from clients and suddenly, *bam!* Three projects turn up all at once and two of them need to be turned around within 36 hours.

But that, my friends, is the way of the freelance lifestyle—and if you want to make it in the world of being a home-based small business owner, you have to adapt quickly to being flexible, available, and saying "yes" a lot, especially for the first couple of years.

Public Service Announcement

The freelancing lifestyle and the life of a home-based small business owner isn't for everyone. It can be extremely rewarding, and when you love it, you will wake up each day with a smile on your face. Passion and enjoyment for your work are crucial to this lifestyle! Be sure that's *you* before making the big leap.

CHAPTER 2: PREPARING FOR THE FREELANCE LIFE & THE STEPS YOU NEED TO TAKE

As mentioned in the Introduction to this book, I spent five months (in my spare time while I still had my day job) preparing for becoming a full-time freelancer. I researched and studied and tried to learn as much as possible during those five months, and I tried to set up my home and mental state for the transition as well. In this chapter, I want to guide you through the steps you need to take to prepare for the freelance life.

One of the few things this book won't cover is the process of setting yourself up as a registered business. The only reason why I have chosen not to address how to do that in this book is because there are so many different types of businesses, and the legalities and requirements differ slightly based on the type you choose to have.

Instead, I recommend that you speak with an accountant immediately. A good accountant can help you understand what you need to know about getting a registered business number, and they can advise you on the type of business that makes the most sense for the work you will be doing. You will also be extremely grateful for having a good accountant when tax season comes around! When you run your own business, tax time can be complicated. Don't make it harder on yourself by trying to do your taxes yourself. Invest in your business and yourself by hiring an accountant to deal with all of that for you. Trust me, you will *not* regret it.

You may also wish to have a meeting with a lawyer to ensure you have all of your bases covered (this might be especially useful for liability insurance when it comes to writing online, for example).

Setting yourself up as a registered business is definitely one of the most important things when it comes to starting your business. But there are other important things you'll need to take care of before you launch your business—let's dive into it.

Physical Preparation

This is the obvious stuff, and often the easiest to prepare for as well. As a freelance writer or editor, you will need all the basics for your home office. Here are some of my essentials:

- **A good table and chair, plus a standing desk.** I was lucky that there was a gigantic design table in my condo when I first moved in. I use it as a standing desk, and find that I actually write better when I'm standing—something about being on your feet provides healthy energy flow for the creative processes. But I can't stand all day long! That's where a good (regular) desk with a comfortable chair comes in handy. I often switch between the two desks multiple times each day to maximize my energy and productivity.

- **A computer.** Much as I love handwriting things, my hands cramp way faster when I handwrite compared to typing. Plus, typing is so much faster! Got to get those thoughts onto paper as soon as possible. I recommend getting a laptop rather than a desktop computer so you can move from one work station to another, and so you can work from anywhere: a coffee shop, a different city, etc.

  Along with a computer, it's valuable to have a fast Internet connection at home. You'll need the Internet for fact-checking and research, to connect with clients via email, to update your business website, and to network on social media. Invest in high-speed Internet to reduce frustration and to save on time (if your computer runs slowly or your Internet takes a long time to load, you could lose hours of precious time over the years from just sitting around waiting!).

- **Paper (notebook) and several good-quality pens.** You never know when you'll want to jot something down, and it's good to have a paper and pen handy when you are out for a walk. You'll also want a notebook to bring along to in-person meetings with clients.

  Besides that, make sure the pens you have are ones you love! It's worth investing in a pen that's a little pricier if it feels comfortable to you and if you like the ink style—after all, it's something you could be using every single day.

  In addition to jotting things down throughout the day, another thing I've used a notebook for is my to-do list. When I first started freelancing, I kept a list of about a dozen items I aimed to do each week, and crossed them off as I completed them. Much as I adore my laptop, I prefer to use a pen and paper for this purpose.

- **Red marker and highlighters.** These are essential editing tools. I am a big fan of Track Changes (an editing tool in Word) for editing materials digitally for clients, but when it comes to editing my own writing, I prefer to do it the old fashioned way by printing it out and writing all over it and crossing things out. Moreover, some clients prefer that I do it by hand. Sharpies and different colored highlighters are a must for identifying important things (such as mistakes and inconsistencies).

- **Printer.** I have an all-in-one printer / scanner / photocopier machine, and it is wonderful. You never know when you have to print or scan things (or photocopy them!). Contracts are one of the biggest things you will have to print, sign, and scan back to clients; you might also want to print out online articles you write, for example, to include in your portfolio.

This might not be at the top of the list for a lot of people, but it will make your life as a freelancer so much easier (if only come tax season, when you have to scan a bunch of legal documents so you can email them to your accountant).

- **Dictionary, thesaurus, and style guides.** I have dozens of books on writing and editing. I love my Canadian Oxford Dictionary and Chicago Manual of Style—those are probably my two most-used books. But every collection can use a little Kenneth Burke, too!

Depending on the type of writing and / or editing you intend on doing or specializing in, you will want different types of style guides and reference materials (and even dictionaries, if you are editing for people in different countries. I have edited for Canadian English, US English, and UK English, for example). These can get pricey, so be choosy on your initial selections. You can build your library over time as your needs change and evolve.

- **Smartphone and / or agenda.** Smartphones are becoming the norm, but they really are wonderful and worth mentioning for keeping track of your work. You can keep all of your tasks in your smartphone calendar (sync it up to your Google calendar as well!) and set up Alerts to remind you of meetings and deadlines. Even if you prefer to use a paper agenda, it's not a bad idea to track things on your smartphone as a backup.

- **Business cards.** This is a must! Your business cards don't have to be fancy, either. They should state your name, phone number, email address, website, and your title (such as "freelance editor").

When it comes to business card design, opt for simplicity first. You can always choose crazy colors and add images in the future if you really want to, but I recommend going for an understated look. It will showcase you as a professional, which is something you will need to highlight in the beginning when you're new to the industry. Fonts such as Helvetica, Arial, or Times New Roman are classic choices; choose fairly neutral, basic colors as well if you're going for that professional feel.

You can get nice, inexpensive business cards from online companies such as BuildASign and Vistaprint. If you have design skills, by all means create your own design (and if you're new to design, you can always try your hand at it in PicMonkey). I had my first business cards designed and printed at my local UPS store. It was a little pricey, but they were lovely cards and worth every penny. Be realistic about how much you want to spend on business cards; I've had cards from BuildASign and Vistaprint as well, and there is nothing wrong with those options.

- **To-do lists, checklists, and tracking tools.** I mentioned this briefly above when it comes to using a paper and pen, but I recommend you figure out a way of managing your projects and time that *works for you*.

I transitioned from writing lists in a notebook, to writing my tasks out on a weekly sticky notepad (which I stick to my desk each week right by my computer), to marking everything down on a whiteboard, to my most recent favorite way of managing projects: using a "daily maintenance" checklist, which I keep in a clear plastic sheet protector and use a dry-erase marker to check things off throughout the day.

I love this daily maintenance checklist as a tool because it saves me on *so much paper* that I otherwise would have gone through. But it's better to use this tool after you've been working for a while, or when you have a lot of ongoing, long-term work to keep track of, so that you know what kinds of tasks you have to do every single day or every week. At this time, I still use my weekly sticky notepad too for any short-term or one-off projects.

I find my daily maintenance checklist most valuable for managing my blog and the social media for my business, as well as managing social media for clients. You can see a sample template of a daily maintenance checklist in Appendix VIII.

- **A website.** How will people find you if you don't have a website? I'm a big fan of using Wordpress.org, because it allows you to easily use the blog feature if you want to incorporate that as part of your business. Use your business name or just your own name as your domain name so people can find your website easily when they search you in Google (and pay the additional fee to get your own domain name and cut out the "wordpress.com" or "blogspot.com" section from the end—it will look much more professional if it's "YourName.com" vs. "YourName.wordpress.com," for example).

  At the very least, your website should include your contact information, a bio with your work experience / education, the services you offer, a professional photograph of you, and a list of projects you have worked on in the past, as well as some testimonials (plus a portfolio—see more on that below). Adding a blog component to your website can also be a great way to get on a more personal level with potential clients, and help them get to know you.

As this book isn't about setting up a website, I won't go into much further detail about getting a website here—you can visit Wordpress.org to find all the information you need and get started.

- **A portfolio.** Depending on how much freelancing (or just plain writing and editing) you have done in the past, your portfolio could be of all different sizes. If you have a sample of just three or four pieces, that's still a good start!

  Having an online portfolio as a PDF (with your name and website in the header or footer), as well as a print portfolio in a binder (using sheet protectors and labels with publishing dates, as well as a copy of your resume / bio / contact information), will do nicely in this case. Including testimonials on both your online and your print portfolio is even better.

  You might not end up ever needing to use your print version, but it's handy to have. Bring it along to meetings just in case your prospective client asks to see examples of past work.

  Make it easy to access your online portfolio on your website by having a whole section dedicated to your portfolio. Keeping it in a Word document and saving it as a PDF is an easy to way to upload it, but if you want it to look a little fancier, you can use a design program such as InDesign or even use some kind of Prezi platform. Just make sure you don't sacrifice professionalism for an interesting presentation display.

I recommend clearing out a specific space in your home just for office work and your business. It can make a big difference in terms of that "going to the office" feel, and for focusing on your work if distractions are a problem. The nice thing is that when your office is in your home, you can personalize it just the way you like! Get your favourite colors and photographs in there and prepare it to be your official, professional workspace.

Some of the things to think about when preparing your workspace are the colors you choose (orange, for example, is a color that stimulates creativity, which is why I've used it as my computer desktop background), and the organization of the space. You want your workspace to be well-organized so that you are never distracted about tidying it when you are supposed to be working.

Dust your desk regularly and remove clutter as much as possible. Put papers and books in their proper places each night so that when you start your workday the following morning, it will be tidy, clean, and ready for you to get started working. Do whatever you can to eliminate distractions in your workspace.

Mental Preparation

You might want to roll your eyes at this section—but you really do need to prepare yourself mentally! As a freelancer, you must rely on your own self-discipline to find clients and complete work. When people find out that I am a freelancer, one of the many reactions I get is, "oh, I could *never* do that—on the rare occasion that I work from home, I get too distracted by Facebook!"

As an entrepreneur, a business owner, or a freelancer (call yourself what you like), you need to be able to prevent yourself from being distracted. In the time leading up to your freelancing career, check in with yourself. Be honest with yourself about your ability to settle down and get to work when *you* are the boss. Are you prepared to work in the evenings and on weekends? Are you prepared to get out there and find your own clients? Are you prepared to learn how to network? Are you prepared to handle the stress and anxiety that can come with not knowing when your next paycheque will be arriving?

In addition to preparing your own mental state, you need to prepare the people you live with for the transition, too. They need to understand that you can't start taking on all of the household chores and errands just because you're working from home now. Unless they have experience working from home as well, you will likely need to have several conversations with them about how when you are at home working, you are *working*.

Friends and family who you don't live with might have to be told this several times, too. Prepare yourself to hear from a lot of people that "it must be nice not to have to work!" or that "I wish I could sit at home all day, too!" or that "I really need XYZ to be done but I can't do it because I have to be at work all day—can you run the errand for me instead?"

The more you can explain what the freelance life entails to other people, the more they will understand that you aren't "unemployed." I happen to have been very lucky in this scenario (particularly because I don't have children or pets, and my common-law husband was already accustomed to working from home because he was doing his Master's at the time that I started freelancing) and didn't have to deal with this issue too much, but it's best to understand what *could* happen when you start freelancing. Prepare yourself and your loved ones for it!

Financial Preparation

All of the literature on freelancing will tell you to save up at least six months' worth of expenses before quitting your day job. I didn't do that.

Now, in a way I would definitely recommend that this is a "do as I say, not as I do" situation—in other words, even though I didn't save up six months' worth of expenses, *it's still the right thing to do*. Having six months' worth of expenses will prepare you for if you don't make enough money in the first few months to pay for bills and living expenses, and it will also provide you with a buffer to pay for things like continuing education.

On the other hand, even though I gambled, it paid off. Here's why:

- **I've always been good at paying off credit card bills.** I knew that if I got up to $5,000 on my credit card, it would be unfortunate, but it wouldn't be the end of the world because my credit rating had always been awesome—and at the very least, I could always pay triple the minimum (which is a good secret to keep in mind: don't just pay the minimum! Your interest rates will be so high that the minimum won't add anything toward the balance you actually have to pay off. Instead, pay *at least* triple the minimum so you can chip away at the actual balance).

  If I truly couldn't find work in the first couple months, I knew it could start flooding in later on (remember that freelancers tend to have feast-or-famine situations), and then I'd be able to pay off that credit card and then some. Moreover, I made the transition from my 9–5 job to being a full-time freelancer during tax season, when I was expecting a nice tax return (one of the benefits of working for a charity meant that I was used to working on a shoestring budget!). There couldn't have been a more perfect time for that tax money to come in and provide a nice buffer while I got on my feet.

- **I had multiple back-up plans.** Yes, you can rely on your credit card— but don't rely on it so much that you pile up the debt. Having a few other options for getting paid work is a more financially-smart decision. I had many back-up plans in place and different businesses where I knew that I could apply for work for a short period of time (even if it meant going into an industry I didn't want to be in, such as working as a server or a cook) if things didn't go as planned.

  One of the keys with back-up plans is to *make them available, without being appealing.* That way, you'll know that if things don't go as you hope, you still have somewhere to turn… but since you won't *want* to turn to it, you know that you'll be working extra hard to *make it* as a freelancer.

- **I watched my bank account daily.** As a freelancer, you should keep track of exactly how much you make and exactly how much you spend. I knew how much I needed to pay the bills and still enjoy myself (such as going out for dinner). I kept an eagle eye on my bank account so I knew what I was spending things on and where I could cut back when necessary, and I kept every penny of income and expenses in an Excel spreadsheet to track it all.

  If a spreadsheet on your computer isn't quite your thing, you could also take advantage of websites and apps that offer budgeting software, such as <u>Mint.com</u>. The important thing is to track your finances and be aware of your income and spending habits.

- **I *did* have savings.** Although I didn't have much in my chequing account, I had some money tied up with investments and a savings account with my investment company. It wasn't money that I wanted to touch until retirement, but I knew that if I *really* had to, I *could* use that money.

  In addition, I had been putting money away in a jar every week since January 2014. By summer 2014, I had more than $1,000 cash in a jar. I wanted to save it up for a nice trip somewhere, but it was fantastic to know that if things got really tight, I always had that to rely on (*before* moving to a job outside my industry)—luckily, I never have had to access any of those savings.

  Besides these kinds of savings, it's a good idea to set up a tax-free savings account that you can contribute to bi-weekly so you have some flexibility with spending (I recommend setting this account up to automatically withdraw $25–$40 a couple times each month), or to have a cash budget for entertainment, for example. Make sure you have a budget for those things you love to do, like going out to the movie theatre—set aside a small amount of money for the simple pleasures in life.

- **I didn't have a lot of monthly expenses.** I can get by with spending just $2,000 / month for everything from mortgage to groceries to a little fun spending money. This means that I didn't really have to make *that* much to pay my bills in the first few months, which was a relief and made finding work a little less intimidating… and since I was quitting a job where I'd only been making $16 / hour, it wasn't as though I was missing out on a really great paycheque.

If you are going into the freelancing business, you have to be prepared to look at your bank account daily. You have to be smart enough to put money aside when you make a lot, because there *will* be slow times with your business. You have to be okay with potentially picking up some lacklustre jobs on the side in the beginning.

Although the financial side of freelancing can be scary, remember that **being a freelancer is one of the most low-risk types of entrepreneurship out there.** You probably already have a desk in your home, a laptop, and a few basic office supplies. As a freelancer, you don't have to worry about a huge amount of overhead costs: if you work from home, you don't need to rent out office space, and you also won't need to worry about paying employees, purchasing product to sell, and so on. You really just have to worry about basic living expenses and some professional learning costs. The financial risk of freelancing doesn't seem quite as scary anymore, now does it?

One of the most important things is to learn how to budget and manage your income and expenses—and stick to your budgeting plan (more about this in Appendix VI)! Identify ways that you can cut back on spending in preparation for potential lean times as a freelancer. Your first six months could be pretty tight when it comes to finances, and you will likely spend much more of your time looking for work rather than actually *doing* paid work for clients. If you plan ahead, are careful with your money, and *hustle* to get work, there is no reason why you shouldn't succeed as a freelancer.

Ultimately, before you become a full-time freelancer, you really *should* have money set aside for your freelancing business. For me, I got out of my day job when I did because I had a little bit of money set aside and I was so unhappy with my day job that I absolutely *had* to get out of there, but I wouldn't necessarily recommend that as a business strategy.

Time Management and Project Preparation

One of the last components that you need to prepare for, when it comes to the freelance life, is managing your time well. If you've been able to answer "yes" to the above questions in the Mental Preparation section, you're off to a good start!

As a freelancer and home-based business owner, you will need to be well-disciplined. You have to be excellent at time management in order to succeed.

Spending my down time and slow business days on ongoing projects and business administration / maintenance has been extremely valuable for me. Use your down time as catch-up time! Spend your slow days on routine maintenance tasks such as writing and scheduling articles on your website, promoting and marketing your business, and working on long-term projects.

I made a name for myself by specializing in rush jobs. Some of my clients have come to appreciate me and keep coming back to me in part because of the quality of work that I churn out, but also because of how *quickly and efficiently* I complete projects. **If you excel at time management, make a point of getting work turned around in half the time promised (without sacrificing quality, of course!).**

Something else, which you can only learn about yourself over time, is knowing approximately how long a project will take. I remember taking on one project on a Sunday afternoon which I suspected I could complete in the space of two hours (the project was also a rush job). After the first hour, I immediately contacted my client and informed her that I had completely underestimated the time, and that it would take closer to eight hours. Since she was paying for the project by the hour, it was extremely important that she was aware of the difference in time and therefore the difference in the fee. As it happened, this wasn't a problem for her, and so I spent most of Sunday evening working on the project and submitted it late Monday morning.

In another scenario, I thought a project would take me about 15 hours, when it took me about four times that long. I was being paid a flat rate, and therefore ended up making below minimum wage per hour on that project.

I tell you the above stories to illustrate how some jobs, which seem fairly simple and straightforward, can take much more time than you suspect. **As much as you can, overestimate how long it will take you to complete the project.** If you say it will take you 10 hours and you can return the project within the week, imagine how pleased your client will be if it only ends up taking you seven hours and you can return it within three days.

The important thing to keep in mind here is that a) you should never sacrifice quality work for returning projects quickly, and b) you never know when complications with the project may arise or when some kind of crisis might occur (for example, your computer crashing—AHHH!). Before quoting times and fees, always think it through very carefully. I cannot stress this enough.

Setting Fees

I did so much research on how to set rates in the months leading up to becoming a full-time freelancer. It is frustrating, because some resources provide a complicated formula, or a resource might say to do $15 / hour while another says $300 / hour, or one source might recommend charging by the hour and another will tell you vehemently that you should ONLY do project-based set fees.

Figuring out how to set your rates is exhausting!

Since starting full-time freelancing, I have worked anywhere from $10 / hour to $100 / hour. Sometimes I'll charge by the hour; other times, I'll do a flat rate.

My recommendation is to **charge by the hour in the beginning.** You'll be able to better gauge how long projects will take, and you won't make your client pay far more than is necessary (or hurt yourself by taking much longer than you expected).

Within a few months of full-time freelancing, I thought I knew what I was doing. I was confident I had a good handle on setting rates, and I agreed to do some ghostwriting for a client. She had an extremely tight budget, and our fee was around $300. I knew it was a miniscule amount compared to most ghostwriting projects (which can be upwards of $10,000), but I was also in need of cash, and it was an interesting project.

She was a great client to have, but the project ended up being *far* more complicated than I had anticipated. By the time I told her that I simply couldn't do any more work for her, I had spent something in the area of 60 hours working on the project. Ouch.

She paid me and provided me with a nice testimonial, and it was a great experience because I learned some important lessons from it! But it is definitely something I have no desire to repeat again.

Here are my recommendations when it comes to setting rates:

- **Charge by the hour for most writing and editing projects.** This keeps it nice and easy for tracking the time you spend, and you won't have to worry about calculating some big formula. Moreover, it can be less intimidating for clients when you put it as, for example, $50 / hour, rather than $1,000 for the project. Of course, it's a good idea to provide your client with a rough estimate for how long it will take you to complete the project—or keep them posted throughout (for example, once you've hit the 5-hour or 10-hour mark and you're only a quarter of the way through the project) to help them understand what the total cost will be. Always be upfront with a client as soon as you know how much it will cost them.

- **Charge by the project for writing and editing projects that are similar to what you've worked on in the past, or for projects that require skills you are especially strong in, or for social media work.** If you know roughly how long it will take you to work on a project, or if you're especially skilled in the area you're being hired for, it's cheating yourself if you complete high-quality work too quickly. Most clients will be happy to pay $100 for editing a short project that might only actually take you 40 minutes, for example. Can you imagine if you'd charged by the hour for that, and your rate was $30 / hour? Don't devalue yourself!

Charging by the hour is also a good idea if you're doing any social media management or consulting. I'm adding this one in here because if you are a freelance writer and editor, in this day and age, I'd be very surprised if you don't end up doing some amount of social media work for clients at some point. Charging by the hour doesn't make sense for social media, because social media is one of those things that you need to constantly be doing and be aware of.

It might only take you five minutes to write a Tweet, but what about the time spent connecting with other followers, reviewing analytics, creating images, finding other posts to ReTweet, answering inquiries, and putting together schedules, to name just the tip of the iceberg when it comes to social media management? You will probably also have to do some social media on short notice or in the evenings and on weekends, and you should be compensated fairly for that.

Charging by the hour is difficult to calculate for social media, so I recommend just not doing it altogether! (And if you're looking at a starting point for how much you should be paid for managing social media for a client—keeping in mind that the scope of the project and the amount of work involved and your experience etc. are all important factors to consider—I'd recommend charging anywhere between about $200–$600 per month, per social media platform.)

- **As a general rule, $30–$60 / hour is a good range for most free-lancers.** Remember how I told you at the beginning of this book that I did some part-time freelancing around the time that I worked for a public relations company? Well, I spoke with my boss at the PR company about setting rates as a freelancer, and he recommended that I start out with $40 / hour since I didn't have much experience yet. I stuck with that rate for a couple years before bumping it to $50 / hour. In January 2015 (about five years later), I increased my rate to $60 / hour.

I expect I'll stay at this rate for a while. I like $60 / hour, because it provides me with a good return on my time, and it's also a reasonable amount for most clients that I want to work with. I anticipate that if I increase my fees again (which I would probably only do after another couple of years, and only once I've taken professional courses to enhance existing skills or develop news ones), I would still keep my fee at $60 / hour for clients I already have a good relationship with, for example.

Keep in mind that hourly rates change depending on the economic situation and even the city you work in. But if you're doing work for clients in other cities (or countries), then this will be a moot point. If you have minimal experience, start at around $30; if you have more experience in your field, or if you specialize in rush jobs, charge closer to $50 from the beginning.

- **Pick a number and stick to your guns.** Some clients will think $15 / hour is too much. Others might be amazed at your *low low price!* of $100 / hour. Someone is always going to question your rates. Sometimes, you just need to choose a number and be confident that *it* is the amount that you're worth.

This doesn't mean you can't negotiate, however. If you get along with a client and you like the project and their budget allows for $30 / hour instead of your usual $40 / hour rate, I say, go for it! That person might continue to provide you with more work, pass on your name to their colleagues, give you a great testimonial, or pay you more on the next project.

One of my clients, who has become a friend of mine, works with non-profit organizations. That means her budget is generally fairly small, and she can usually only pay me about half of my usual rate. However, she continues to come back to me with more work, we have a fantastic relationship, I enjoy the work she gets me to do, it's all for a good cause, and she often has enough hours for me that I get quite a nice cheque by the end of the project. It is a pleasure working with her and it is totally worth my time and energy to take on the projects she gives to me.

One final note: you don't necessarily need to put your rates on your website and set them in stone! Your rate might vary drastically from one client to the next, and that's okay.

Do some research on your own, by all means, but the above is really the basics that will get you started with setting your rates.

CHAPTER 3: CREATING YOUR BUSINESS STRATEGY & BUILDING YOUR NETWORK

Before you begin writing and editing for clients, you need to find clients—and in order to do that, you need to put together and create a business strategy, as well as build your network!

This can be challenging, and you might want to pass it by, but having a business strategy is an absolute necessity for ensuring the success of your business. One of the primary reasons why freelancing didn't work for me the first time I tried it was because I was getting clients based on pure chance and happening to be at the right place at the right time. That sort of "strategy" works for a little while, but eventually it's going to come back to bite you! You *must* have a strategy in place and a plan to follow when you are starting your own business.

What You Need to Think About When Creating Your Business Strategy

Starting your own business can feel rather overwhelming. That's why I like to start by creating a to-do list. Just start writing down all of the things you can think of that you need to do before launching your business. This will be a working list and you'll likely add to it and check things off over the next few months.

Some of the things you might include in your to-do list are updating (or creating!) your website, putting together a portfolio of writing samples, and getting business cards printed, for example. These are all random things, and this list can be stapled to the back of your business strategy once you've put it together. I like to have everything laid out on paper so I can think clearly—it might work well for you, too.

Now it's time to really get started with putting together your business strategy. Keep in mind that you want to be explicit, clear, and specific on all the details.

For example, you might say that your goal is to make $4,000 / month with your business. But rather than just leave it at that, you should also detail in your strategy *when* you hope to start making that amount and the breakdown of the type of work you will need to do to make that kind of money. Your business strategy might change over time—it's certainly not set in stone—but the more details you can include at the beginning, the more securely you can set yourself up for success.

Here are the key components you need to include in your business strategy:

- **Business name, industry, and mission statement.** I kept things simple in terms of my business name—it's just Sagan Morrow. This makes my life so much easier because I *am* my brand; people see my name or my business name and they instantly make the connection. There is no question of "who is running the XYZ company?" when your name *is* the company. Of course, if you intend to hire more people as part of your business, you might want to give it a different name than your own name. Take some time to seriously think about it before jumping in.

  The mission statement should describe what your business does and also include your values (for example, are there certain organizations you will or will not work for?). Write out your mission statement in just one or two sentences to keep it clear and concise. You might need to write it out several times before you get it just right.

One way you can do this is to write a full page of your values and a description of your business: then, you can pull the main pieces from that and succinctly write your brief mission statement. (Keep a copy of the longer version with your to-do list at the back of your business strategy! It could be a great resource to have easily accessible).

- **Business goals.** What do you want to achieve with your business? Where do you see yourself in five years? Write down your vision, and be sure to use the SMART (specific, measurable, attainable, realistic, and timely) method.

  Be sure to include a variety of goal *types* here, too: three-month goals, six-month goals, one-year goals, two-year goals, three-year goals, five-year goals, and 10-year goals, for example (you don't have to do ALL of these, but choose at least a few!).

  Hold off on your financial goals (we'll get to that part later in your business plan)—instead, for this section focus on including goals around the type of clients you want to have, the exact type of work you want to be doing (your "dream work,"), professional and skills development / education goals, networking goals, etc. Don't rush this stage, and don't be afraid to dream big!

- **Target audiences.** Who is your target audience? Who do you want as clients? Who will benefit from your services? Who will *want* or require your services? What are the demographics of these people? Be as specific as possible here, because it will help you with the next section.

- **Marketing strategy.** Once you have identified your target audience(s), you need to know where to find those people! Do your research to determine where they are and the best way to market to them. Different social media platforms cater to different audiences, and one or several of these might be a good primary marketplace. Networking events and distributing flyers are other common marketing practices.

In your marketing strategy, include where your audience is, how you will get there, and the ways you will market to them (from online marketing to print marketing to network marketing etc.). Try to estimate how long it will take you to conduct your marketing each day or each week, and make marketing a major priority, especially in the beginning.

If you want to market online, for example, you can't just build a website and then wait for people to come to you! You have to create good content and use a beautiful, professional design on your website; you have to comment on other people's blogs, follow people on social media, and interact with people across a variety of social media platforms. You might have to learn SEO and explore ways to encourage people to sign up for your email list and participate in forums. Plan ahead when it comes to marketing.

• **Work plan.** This is an important one that will likely change dozens of times over your freelancing career, but it's good to start out with a rough plan. Estimate how many hours each day and each week you will work; plan for what time you will start your day, the types of activities you'll conduct in the morning compared to the afternoon, and how long you want or need to spend on various activities each week (for example, business administration, researching your industry, marketing your business, searching for and building relationships with potential clients, and doing the actual work for clients).

If you don't have a work plan or daily schedule to adhere to, you might fall into the trap of whiling away the hours without accomplishing much. Too many new freelancers fail because they sleep in, lounge around with their coffee, and do only a little work here and there. If you have never freelanced before, you'll be better off to give yourself some kind of structure in the beginning! You might discover that you are more productive without a solid structure, but you have to get into the habit of being disciplined and somewhat structured before you can experiment with different working styles if you want to be successful.

- **Budget.** Include here how much you intend on spending in a year on professional development and business expenses. The first couple years, you might want to set aside up to 20% of your income on professional development and business expenses (including memberships to relevant organizations, conference registration, website upkeep, etc.). In later years, you might want to reduce that amount to around 10%, for example.

It really depends on your current level of skills and your current resources as to the percentage amount that you should spend on professional development: if you want to be a freelance editor but you haven't actually taken any courses in editing and you don't have any idea how to run a small business, you might need to spend up to 40% of your income that first year in diving into courses, text books, workshops, and so on to hone your skills and build your knowledge base. The important thing is to know where your money is going, and to spend your income on things that will be useful to your business.

Your marketing budget will vary depending on where your target audiences are. Traditional marketing, such as print ads, can be expensive. On the other hand, many demographics use social media, so it may be more cost-effective to do that. Regardless, don't forget about marketing when you put together your budget.

You will ultimately have to figure out what percentage makes the most sense based on your background, lifestyle, and income, but keep in mind that what you spend on professional development and business expenses should be an investment in your future. Think carefully about where you want to spend your money and how you want to spend it, and how spending that money now will pay off in the future.

- **Financial goals.** It's nice to think that you'll make enough money in the first few months to pay for all of your bills, and while it's certainly not impossible, it is unlikely. When I started freelancing full-time, I created a financial goal for each month for the next year, and I didn't expect to start making enough to cover all of my bills completely until I had been freelancing for six months. As it happened, I made more than I was expecting for the first and third months—the second, fourth, and fifth months, on the other hand, were a little lean. But that is the freelance life! It goes up and down, and it's all about the averages as time goes on.

So: how do you create a financial goal?

Start out by understanding how much money you need each month to live on. Let's say that the bare minimum you need for your living expenses is $2,000 / month. In that case, you probably want to be making about $2,000 / month within the first six months. Therefore, you might have goals to make a quarter or half that amount for the first three to four months, and then that full amount by the six-month mark.

Then, you'll want to make *more* than your minimum amount to account for lean times and for savings and flexibility in life choices. Perhaps that means your ultimate goal is to make $5,000 / month for a respectable salary of $60,000 / year. In that case, consider how long it took you to make your minimum amount, and estimate how quickly you'll be able to increase that sum in the coming months.

Your broad goals might include the following:

- 3-month mark: $1,000 / month
- 6-month mark: $2,000 / month
- 1-year mark: $3,000 / month
- 1.5-year mark: $4,000 / month
- 2-year mark: $5,000 / month

I recommend being very specific with the in-between months, too. Otherwise, you might discover that the time goes by much faster than you expected! Give yourself specific financial goals every single month for the first couple of years so you effectively keep on top of your finances.

One more note when it comes to finances: don't worry if your income fluctuates a lot in your first year. That's totally normal for freelancers. It's more important to look at averages over time.

So, are you ready to create your business strategy? Jump to Appendix III for a template of a business plan that you can use as a starting point for your own strategy.

Practical Ways to Build Your Online Network

To get clients, you need to have a network. If you're an introvert like me (which many freelancers are—and which can actually make it easier for transitioning to freelancing because freelancing can involve a lot of alone time), networking can be a challenging activity! It can just take so much energy out of you, which is counterintuitive to being able to really work the room the way you need to, when you're trying to promote your business.

One of the ways you can get around this issue is to enhance your online presence and build your network online. Connecting with people over the Internet doesn't have the same effect that networking in person does, so this is a great option if you get drained quickly from the networking environment.

The best social media platform for you depends on who your audience is and which platform they prefer. For myself, I have found that the most effective social media platforms for business are LinkedIn and Twitter. Facebook, Pinterest, and Instagram can also be very useful sources, depending on how you go about marketing through them. It comes down to knowing where your audience is, and also to identifying the type of network that *you* prefer and excel at.

There are a few key ways to effectively use social media as a networking tool:

- **Engage in social media every day.** I spend a good hour in total each day, at least five days each week, checking up on social media and updating it. I often check it first thing in the morning and then frequently throughout the day. Consistency is so important because by being a "regular feature" on someone's newsfeed, they will come to recognize you and build trust in what you say. This strategy builds your reputation and enhances your credibility. Moreover, these people will be that much more likely to think of you when they have work that requires services you offer!

- **Get the conversation going.** The word "social" in social media is important! Connect with others, respond to what they say, ask questions, and enjoy some good dialogue. It doesn't have to be about your business or your industry, either: by engaging in a variety of topics and joining in on discussions, you will be able to grow your audience and people will get to see a more personalized side of your business. Post relevant, thoughtful, and engaging content and comments to best build relationships.

- **Use hashtags, images, and links where appropriate.** Although I highly recommend connecting with people in general (not just about things related to your business), you should also include information about your business semi-regularly. Perhaps one to three times each week, if you are posting a couple times each day, for example. When doing so, be sure to link back to your website, use hashtags that will ensure your post reaches more people, and add images to appeal to the broader audience.

And always ensure that you are promoting your business in a *benefits* way. Highlight the benefits that people will get from your services instead of showcasing the features of your service or asking people to support you. On social media, people aren't interested in helping you: they want *you* to help *them!* If you can provide them with interesting resources or materials that are useful to them and solves a problem they have, they will keep coming back to you for more.

How to Network Effectively at In-Person Events

I've attended many networking events in my time, and these are some of the best tips that I have picked up over the years which should be useful for you too:

- **Choose events that make sense.** This one might seem like a no-brainer, but it's really easy to get caught up with the idea that we should constantly attend networking events... and then end up attending events that don't actually do anything for us. The events themselves should be related to your industry, or the event attendees should be your target audience.

- **Go with a game plan in mind.** If you attend the event without having a goal in mind, you are going to walk away with nothing. Prepare yourself ahead of time by creating intentions for yourself. What are three things you will do at this event? Who are three types of people you want to connect with? What will you walk away with at the end of the event?

- **Sometimes it's easiest to attend the event by yourself.** It's tempting to bring along a friend or a spouse to these types of things, but in my experience, it just makes me less inclined to start talking to other people besides them. Go by yourself to give you that extra push you need to strike up conversation with complete strangers.

- **...But you can also effectively network with another freelancer.** The trick to going to events with other people for networking purposes is to go with *colleagues* rather than, for example, your spouse. That way, you can be each other's business wingman! When you attend an event with a colleague, you know that you are both there to meet other people, and you can also help to promote each other's business, or just spend time together if the event turns out to be totally different than what you had expected.

- **Networking is less intimidating when you know there's a timeframe involved or when you are "forced" together.** Is everyone sitting at tables? Great—pick a table and start talking to the people there. Will a speaker be presenting in five minutes? Now is the time to start talking to someone! You will feel much more comfortable if you know there is a time limit on your conversation or if you are sitting next to someone who doesn't have anyone to talk to (except for you, now!).

- **If the event has a hashtag or a list of attendees, connect with some people ahead of time.** I love this strategy. I was recognized at one conference because I had done this very thing. All you need to do is Retweet what an attendee said or engage with them in some other way on social media—when you see each other at the event and recognize their names from the name tags, it will feel almost like you already know each other, and take some of the pressure off.

- **Don't worry about spending too much time talking to one person, if you're having a good, meaningful conversation that is of value to you.** In all the rules of networking, one of the things people talk about the most is that you shouldn't spend more than a couple minutes talking to one person before moving to the next. I disagree with this. If we're talking about building long-term, lasting relationships, as well as getting people to think about you at a later date to hire you or pass your name on to someone else, you have to spend quality time getting to know people.

There is nothing wrong with spending 30 seconds with someone you clearly have nothing in common with, or with spending 30 minutes with someone you "click" with right away. Converse with people at networking events for as long as it feels appropriate.

- **Don't hand out business cards for the sake of handing out business cards.** I see this mistake take place time and time again. People hand out dozens of business cards, and then every single person they give those cards to tosses it in the recycling bin on their way out the door. Be strategic about your business cards. Give them to people whom you genuinely want to connect with later on and will benefit from receiving your card.

Above all, networking is a long game. The payoff can be amazing, but it's about the long-term commitment for maximum success. It might take two weeks of publishing and commenting on social media for two hours a day, every day, before you get a client out of it, or it might take six months. Likewise, you could attend eight networking events and not get a single client—but you might get three clients out of the ninth event. Or one of those people you spoke with might contact you a year later with a job. Or they might pass your name or business card on to someone else, and three months down the road you'll get work out of it.

The important thing to keep in mind here is that **networking works**, but it takes time, patience, and effort, and you might not always see the results of it immediately. By continuing to network on a regular basis, you *will* get clients.

The Case for Leaving People "Wanting More" at Networking Events

The people I most often want to connect with at events aren't necessarily the ones who I've had long discussions with in the past. Instead, the people I'm keen to connect with are the ones who I've only had the chance to meet briefly at a previous event, but the conversation we had was awesome before it was interrupted. I want to know more about that person and I want to chat with them again!

That's why it can be a great idea to find a reason to graciously end a conversation before covering all of your talking points. This person will want to speak with you again next time, or they'll want to have your business card so they can connect with you on social media. You wouldn't have that same eagerness if you tell them everything about you and all of your best stories the very first time you meet them!

CHAPTER 4: LAUNCHING YOUR FREELANCE WRITING & EDITING BUSINESS

You have completed your business plan, you've done your research on the industry, and now you are ready to actually launch your business and start getting paid projects—congratulations! In this chapter, we'll address every step you need to take to successfully launch your business.

Choosing Your Launch Date

It's a good idea to have a date set in mind for when you will launch your business, just as though you were doing a grand opening for a physical store. Why is this a good idea? Because it will enable you to have a set goal in mind for when you will *complete* all of your preparations and start thinking about your business as a full-time career.

You should also think about this in terms of leaving your current day job. I made the decision to quit my 9–5 job a full five months before my launch date, and I handed in my notice one month before my launch date.

The reason why I chose a launch date that was five months down the road was for a couple of reasons: first, it was the same time my contract would be up for renewal and it seemed the most appropriate and fair to the organization I was working with to leave at that point; second, my day job was very stressful and exhausting, so there was a limit on how much time I could give each week to prepare for making the transition (and therefore I needed the extra couple of months to do my research and ensure all preparations were underway); and third, I wanted to have time to save up some money, since I wasn't sure how much I would be bringing in once I started freelancing.

Five months was the perfect amount of time for me. I felt very well-prepared for my first day, and the transition went smoothly. Depending on your life and work situation, you might be able to get by with as little as two months of preparation, or you might want to take up to a year to prepare for the launch. But pick a date as soon as you can for the official launch of your business so that you'll start working toward it *now*.

Choosing a specific date for when your business *really* begins will completely switch your mindset from being unemployed or from working in an office to thinking as a full-time freelancer and home-based small business owner. And having that mindset is extremely important if you want to succeed.

Spreading the Word: Word of Mouth

Word of mouth is an amazing way to get started with your business. People who love you and / or love your work can be your greatest assets, and can really help you to expand your business by being your unofficial champions!

Let people know what you are doing and what services you provide clients. If they happen to hear of anyone looking for a writer or editor, they'll be able to pass your name on (and your business card, too). If you are a friendly, approachable person, and if you produce excellent, high-quality work, and you act respectfully and kindly towards your clients, it *will* come back to you in the form of fantastic recommendations.

Much of my work, particularly in the beginning, came through the grapevine via word of mouth. Friends and family will likely be some of your biggest champions, of course, but you'd be surprised at how many other people you're connected with who will end up promoting you, when their goal is to help out their own friends.

Case in point: I've had friends of friends and potential clients pass my name on to *their* friends and colleagues, primarily because *they wanted to do a service for their friend or colleague.* It wasn't so much about "I know a great editor and you should hire her!" as much as it was, "oh, you've finished a manuscript and need an editor? As a matter of fact, I know of one! Here's her contact information." Notice that I also said "potential clients" here: people have passed on my name when we haven't even actually worked together yet! This is where being friendly and genuine comes into play, and why it's also important to have samples of your work online, for instance, so people can see your work even if they don't end up hiring you, for whatever reason.

Word of mouth works. In an effort to help someone else with a problem they're facing, people will indirectly promote you and your services. Thank you, word of mouth!

Spreading the Word: Your Online Networks

Another important way to spread the word is through your online networks. Blogging and social media can be great for letting people know about your work. If you are already a blogger or on social media, you should already have a nice little following, so that will make it much easier for you to promote your work.

I have had old friends and acquaintances on Facebook send me private messages because they saw a status of mine pop up on their newsfeed which was talking about my services and my business, and then they hired me. I've also gotten involved in Twitter chats and used hashtags to connect with authors and business people in my industry whose connections *have the potential* to lead to work down the road. A lot of networking, even in the online communities, is about relationships and thinking long-term.

Tip: If you are spreading the word online (which really, in this day and age, you pretty much have to do), you should also have a great email signature.

I changed mine a lot over the first couple of months as a freelancer, based on what I was seeing other people do and what the research told me. Ultimately, your email signature should include your first and last name, your profession / job title, and a link to your website. You can also include a couple of other key pieces of contact information, such as your email address, phone number, Twitter handle, and LinkedIn page, but try to keep it as short and sweet as possible. If your website has all of that information, then sending people to your website might be the best way to do it. Sometimes providing people with too much information can be overwhelming, in which case you're better off with fewer points of contact.

I always prefer that clients email rather than phone me, so I no longer have my phone number as part of my email signature: just my name, job title, website, and LinkedIn profile. Short and sweet.

Psst... make sure your email signature is professional. Don't use crazy colors. Try to stick with black (or, if you must, dark brown or dark blue). I cringe every time I see a so-called "professional" with a lime green signature (especially when that color doesn't even fit with their company's branding). Just don't do that! Choose a font that is simple and professional, too—no Comic Sans, please.

If you're new to the online world, I recommend you set up a simple Wordpress.org blog and sign up for LinkedIn, at the very least. Add other social media platforms if you are willing to spend the time and energy on it and if your clients are there, but don't get on a bunch of social media platforms just because other people say it's a good idea. Engage those critical thinking skills and evaluate if it would really be valuable for you, your business, and your audience.

The Basics of Blogging

How exactly can I spread the word about my business through my blog, you might ask? This can be a little more delicate! Depending on your blog theme, you might be able to start talking about your business fairly frequently (for example, if your blog is all about providing writing advice and you're providing writing services, the two go hand in hand). If the topic of your blog doesn't have anything to do with your business, you'll have to be creative in figuring out how to mesh the two. Remember that you don't need to include information on your business in every blog post; the odd mention or link here and there will suffice.

If you are just starting out with writing a blog, choose a topic that fits with your business. You'll be able to provide a service to people while promoting your business simultaneously. That's a good marketing choice right there.

When you are blogging for business purposes, here are a few key things to take into consideration:

- **Sidebar widgets can strategically be very good for business.** I am a huge proponent of learning basic coding so you can create your own little widgets and mini advertisements for your business. Wordpress.org makes life easy with its widget system, and you can add all kinds of things once you've installed the right plugins.

    Create an ad for your testimonials page, install widgets for your social media newsfeeds, offer a blog or newsletter subscription button, and so on. Think strategically about what you *really* want your reader to look at and to do when they arrive at your blog—and use that as your call to action in your sidebar.

    A great basic widget, for making a clickable image in your sidebar, is to use the following code (replacing the sections in caps with your own words, of course):

    <a href="URL YOU WANT IMAGE TO LINK TO" title="ANY TITLE YOU WANT"></a>

- **Always ensure there are sharing buttons on every blog post.** If readers like your work, make it easy for them to share it. If they can't find the right button within about three seconds, that might be enough to prevent them from sharing an article, even if they really like it. Don't let this opportunity pass you by! Install social media sharing buttons on every blog post and in your blog's sidebar, and make them BIG so people can find them immediately.

  There are plenty of plugins on Wordpress.org that make adding sharing buttons easy, and you can also choose which social media platforms to show. The basics, like Twitter, Facebook, Pinterest, and LinkedIn, are must-haves. Other ones that you choose are purely a personal preference and should be based on what platforms your audience is most likely to use.

- **Review your "About" pages regularly.** For the first few years that I blogged, I was notorious for writing something on my About page and then forgetting all about it. But here's the thing: the About page is the *first* page your readers will check out when they visit your website. Take care to update that page regularly and to make it visually appealing. Ensure the content is well-written and fairly simple and straightforward, as well.

  I recommend skimming your About page at least once a month, if not once a week. You'll constantly see things you can tweak to make it better and better. While you're at it, review the other static pages on your website once a month or so, too: you might have more quotes to add to your testimonials page, or you might need to update your rates on your services page (if you include rates on your website), and so on.

- **Simple is almost always better.** A black background with lime green or even white text over top is going to deter many readers because it's much harder for us to read. Choosing flashy images, pop-up ads, and too much fluff and detail could also potentially lose you a lot of traffic. Instead, go with basic colors that appeal to the eye, and aim for a simple, clean look. Reduce the clutter to keep the readers.

In addition, if you want readers to comment on blog posts, use a regular commenting system. If readers face barriers, such as needing to sign in before commenting, they probably just won't bother to do it at all.

- **When it comes to blog post content itself, make the formatting visually-appealing.** Pepper photographs and images throughout your blog posts and include headings, subheadings, bullets, numbered lists, quotes, etc. Huge chunks of text will cause the reader to skim over your work that much more—which is not ideal.

Now is a good time to mention e-newsletters. Online newsletters can be a useful tool, *if you use them strategically.* Just like anything else on social media, it will only be effective if you take the time and effort to do it right.

The value in an online newsletter is that you have a small following who you *know* is interested in what you have to say, and it can be a fantastic way to stay top of mind to those people every week. I've found it effective to write a once-a-week email featuring previews from the blog posts I wrote that week, as well as a conversational introduction from me and the occasional freebie. Just remember that whatever you choose, you're going to have to stick with it, so give this some time to seriously consider whether or not it's a useful tool for you and your business.

If you are serious about starting an online newsletter as part of the marketing for your business, I recommend checking out the Blog Genie's "First 1,000" e-course to get all the details you need for setting up a newsletter.

Preparing Your Workspace

As mentioned earlier in this book, make sure your workspace is always tidy, clean, and well-organized! Prep your physical workspace with all the tools you need to keep your business running smoothly. Choose items and a space that you feel comfortable with, and in which you can work effectively and productively. You will be spending a lot of time here, so it is worth the extra time, thought, and effort you put into preparing it.

These are some of my must-have tools and elements of a workspace that you might find useful:

- Laptop with a wired mouse (the batteries in my wireless mouse always die fast, so I've gone back to using a wired version).
- Printer (hooked up wirelessly to my computer) with black and colored ink, as well as printer paper.
- A few binders with lined notepaper, page dividers, and clear plastic sheet protectors.
- Stapler and three-hole-punch.
- White board and dry-erase markers.
- Several notebooks and sticky notes.
- Sharpie highlighters and markers.
- Pens (different colors and brands) and pencils.
- Paper clips and bulldog clips.
- Canadian Oxford Dictionary, The Merriam-Webster Dictionary, The Chicago Manual of Style, The Canadian Press Stylebook, and The Lynn Truss Treasury.
- Envelopes (of all sizes) and stamps.
- A variety of different styles and sizes of folders.
- Tape, paper cutter, and paper shredder.

I would recommend that before you jump right into your first day as a full-time freelancer and home-based business owner, you do a little test-run of your workspace. Is everything comfortable? Are you missing crucial writing tools? Does your computer need an update or does your wireless mouse need new batteries? Does it make sense where you have placed everything, or should you rearrange some things to make them easier to access if you use them more frequently than others?

Give it all a spin to ensure it makes you happy and productive—if something doesn't quite work on your test-drive, you will be able to fix it or add to it before your first day so that you can focus completely on your business once you've launched it.

CHAPTER 5: SO YOU'VE LAUNCHED YOUR BUSINESS: NOW WHAT?

Congratulations on launching your business! It's an exciting time to be a freelancer / home-based business owner.

But the hard work isn't over yet...

Three Truths You Need to Know about Being a Freelancer

1. **You can't expect your clients to come to you—you need to always be marketing yourself.**

   YOU are your brand. Whether you are out for coffee with a friend, standing in line at the post office, or running errands at the mall, you should always keep in mind that you are representing your business. How you dress, how you act and react, the purchases you make, the things you say, and the people you associate with are all reflective of who you are, who your brand is, and what your business is all about.

   This isn't a limiting concept, either: in fact, it's a freeing one. When you think about your business as YOU and vice versa, you'll discover that networking and building relationships will take place very organically, and you won't have to worry so much about work / life balance (keep in mind that life is a marathon, not a sprint—it's really about doing <u>what you can, when you can</u>).

Always make sure you have business cards with you, no matter where you are going, and make sure you're carrying your smartphone in case you need to quickly Tweet, Instagram, email, or text. If you see an opportunity arise, put yourself forward. Word of mouth can be a wonderful thing, but *you* have to be at the centre of that little word-of-mouth circle. If you don't let people know who you are and what you do initially, how can they share your business and YOU with other people?

2. **YOU are your business—and that means that you will be putting in a lot of hours.**

At least for the first year, you should expect that you will be living and breathing your business. Of course you should spend time with friends and family and go socializing and take care of your personal life, but you also need to understand that *you* are the one who has to do the work to see the success of your business become a reality. No one else is going to ever care about your business—or you!—as much as you do, and you have to honor that and make it a priority.

As mentioned earlier in this book, for the first year of being a freelancer, you will spend many hours finding clients. That includes networking in person and using social media—during work hours and in the evenings and on weekends. Take advantage of opportunities to connect with new potential clients.

If you are prepared to work long days, evenings, and weekends—maybe not all the time, but a good portion of the time—you will be giving that much more back to your business and reaping the benefits in the future.

3. You have to experiment and try doing things in different ways to see what works best for your business.

I sincerely hope that this book provides you with lots of great ideas to try out for your business, but I'm also aware (and you should be too!) that every business and every businessperson is a little bit different. We all do things in different ways, and testing out a variety of things can enable you to find excellent ways that *work best for you*.

Ultimately, don't be afraid to try something new. Always have a backup plan in case it doesn't work out, but keep in mind that you and your business will never have the opportunity to be the best you can be unless you are willing to take risks and test out doing new things in different ways. As an entrepreneur (which is what you are, as a freelancer!), there will always be some level of risk. Identify what level of risk you're willing to take and put yourself out there.

Being a freelancer isn't easy. It can be stressful, it can mean putting in a lot of hours, it can mean dropping everything for a client, and it can mean some lean times ahead as you try to get on your feet. But the truth is, *being a freelancer can be an amazing experience*. If you are honest with yourself about your work style, your interests, and your ability to mentally, financially, and physically prepare yourself and manage everything throughout your freelancing career, it can be incredibly rewarding.

Freelancing means making your own hours, being your own boss, doing what you love, and working in a place that you feel at home (at least, you should feel at home, since you *are* at home!). Of course, passion for the freelancing life and for your work isn't quite enough. You also need to look for clients and actually get work on a fairly regular, consistent, and long-term basis to succeed.

How to Look for Clients

As a freelancer, you will absolutely need clients. And as mentioned above, your clients aren't necessarily all going to fall in your lap. You have to put yourself out there and find them.

There are a few ways to do this:

- **Networking at in-person events and on social media.** Be sure to choose events which are either relevant to your industry, and / or events which you know potential clients will be attending. If your target audience is on social media (and with social media as prevalent as it is, I'm sure they *are* on social media!), you should be on there and "working the room," too.

  The frequency that you do this will really depend on the type of event and where you're at with needing more work. I would recommend that you do networking online and in-person at least once a week for the first few months, so that you can really get your name out there and start making connections. Visit Meetup. com to find out about some local networking groups relevant to your work near you, or even search on Facebook for local workshops, conferences, and groups of like-minded people.

- **Connect with other freelancers.** In Canada, we have the Editors' Association of Canada, and it's a wonderful opportunity to connect with other editors and build your own little network of connections. The Editorial Freelancers Association is a great resource if you're located in the United States. These types of groups will generally have online forums and offer opportunities to attend events and workshops in your city. Then there are websites like Freelancers Union, which has an amazing archive of fascinating, practical articles that freelancers of all kinds can access for free.

There are groups like this all over—often both national groups and regional ones. Find a group that feels right to you. Even better, if you can build strong relationships with a few others in your field, you can recommend one another to clients if work comes up that isn't quite in your area of expertise or if you're too busy to take on extra work at that time.

- **Word of mouth.** Just like with connecting with other freelancers, if you put yourself out there often enough, people will hear about you! I would say about one-quarter of my work comes from word of mouth, although when I first started, it was more like three-quarters. You shouldn't rely on word of mouth to get you tons of projects, but at the same time, don't underestimate its power. If people like you and the work you do, they will share your name with others – and if people *don't* like you or the work you do, then they'll be vocal about that as well. Always produce quality work and be careful not to burn any bridges.

  Let your friends, family, and past clients know that they can feel free to pass on your name to other people, and that you are available to do more work. I strongly encourage that you say "yes" a lot for your first year of freelancing. Take all the work that you can get to build up your portfolio and job experience. After the first year, you can start to be choosier with your work, but in the beginning, be open to accepting what you can when it's offered to you.

- **Enhance your LinkedIn profile.** I was fortunate early on in my career (just a couple months into being a full-time freelancer) to attend a session on how to optimize your LinkedIn profile by Leslie Hughes of PUNCH! Media at the annual Editors' Association of Canada conference. After following her recommendations (mainly updating my profile, tweaking key words, and participating a lot in group discussions) for just two weeks, my rank jumped from being #132 out of around 180 contacts, all the way up to #18. It was also at this time that a head-hunter contacted me with potential work. After just two weeks! I strongly recommend anyone looking for clients to make themselves a prominent figure on LinkedIn.

I spent close to an hour each day almost every day for those two weeks to make myself a prominent figure. This included updating and tweaking my profile, and finding groups and constructing thoughtful comments to add to discussions. After the first two weeks I began spending less time on LinkedIn—more like 30 minutes, five days each week. If you want to make a big difference fast on LinkedIn, prepare to spend at least that amount of time.

- **Get involved with local small businesses.** You might not get paid a whole lot (one of my gigs with a local business ended up working out to around $5 or $10 per hour in the beginning, although it jumped up to around $40 per hour later on since we had negotiated a flat rate), but you *will* be enhancing your portfolio, supporting the local economy and businesses you believe in, building relationships, and potentially making a lot more money the more you work with them as their business grows. There's also a great sense of community and loyalty with a lot of small businesses, which means you'll probably have strong relationships with the people you work with, and they will likely pass your name on to others.

In fact, that very thing happened with the business I just mentioned; they passed my name on to another local business, which started paying me $1,000 each month (for about 25 hours of work each month) to manage social media. It was definitely worth working for $5–$10 per hour for the first client to get that kind of long-term, sustainable work from the second.

So, how do you get involved with local small businesses? Reach out to them! I am most comfortable on social media, so that's how many of my relationships start. But don't be afraid to drop off your business card at a local business, or to strike up a conversation with the manager at a restaurant you frequent, inquiring as to whether they have ever considered hiring a social media strategist, for example. Think about which local business you would love to work with, what skills you can offer them, and approach them with your idea.

- **Get involved with the local newspaper.** This one falls in line with the above point of connecting with local small businesses, but I want to place it on its own since this book is specifically for writers and editors. Our local university newspaper (the one that I proofread and wrote a column for in university) calls itself a "downtown urban journal," and anyone can work or volunteer for it.

Most of their paid positions are posted at about $100 per week (which amounts to around 10 hours of work each week). This isn't a ton of money, but it certainly counts for something—and again, provides you with that opportunity to build your skills. If you got five or six gigs like this one, it could amount to a full (small) salary. Alternatively, you could volunteer as a regular writer and write articles related to your business, to get your name out there and build your portfolio of experience.

- **Try online freelancing platforms (such as Elance and Freelanced) if you're stuck.** The problem with online freelancing platforms is that they demand a great deal of work from you and pay extremely poorly. But again, it provides you with the opportunity to build your portfolio and resume—and if you're having a tough time paying the bills, every dollar adds up!

If you do choose a freelancing job platform (the one I had the most success with was Elance [now operated by Upwork], but I have to say it's appalling how much of a percentage they take off of your earnings which are already often freakishly low), be smart about it. Submit proposals for projects in which the client has already hired other freelancers and has good reviews on their page.

For the most part, ignore any project that has more than 40 proposals on it already—that's a *lot* of people to compete with. Set aside 20 or 30 minutes each day, if you have the time, to go through all the projects and submit proposals on the ones that look good to you. Just a heads up: a lot of the projects expect you to earn $10 or less per hour. So again, don't waste too much time on this platform.

If you are lucky enough that finances aren't a big concern (for instance, if you live with someone who can pay all the bills), then I would recommend avoiding most online freelancing platforms. Focus much more on building relationships.

Once you have been freelancing full-time for a while and you are meeting your business and financial goals, you can start being choosy about the clients and projects you work with. At this point, go for the ones that really interest you—but note that you will probably not get to this stage until you've been freelancing full-time for a solid year.

Most people starting out as a freelancer won't have that luxury, but even for those of us who start out needing to make money immediately from freelancing should put the effort into the long game. Over time, you'll be able to drop smaller clients and focus more on fewer, bigger clients, if that is your goal.

The LinkedIn Strategy That Got 2 Different Head Hunters Contacting Me in Just 4 Weeks

I never used to really *get* LinkedIn. It was one of those things I had because I'd been told you *should* have it, but I didn't pay too much attention to it... until I sat in on the closing keynote speaker's presentation at the Editors' Association of Canada conference in 2014.

The speaker was Leslie Hughes of PUNCH! Media, and her presentation on the basics of using LinkedIn—including key secrets and strategies that she employs herself—inspired me to take the time to properly learn how to use LinkedIn. I took what I learned from her presentation and combined it with more research that I did, as well as with my own ideas and strategies, to make my LinkedIn profile the best it could be.

My LinkedIn adventure began on June 13, 2014. I ranked 130 out of my 172 connections; in the lower 50%. My goal was rank #10, or to get into the top 5%.

So what did I do?

That first week, I focused on updating my profile to optimize it for LinkedIn. That included updating my photo, volunteer work, summary, and headline. I started following some groups, and even left comments in a couple groups, as well as invited a few people to connect with me. I also shared a status update, commented on an article, and started following a handful of high-profile people. I jumped to #100.

In the second week, when I updated my profile again, invited more people to connect, followed more groups, endorsed some of my connections, commented in groups, and updated my status again, I jumped up to #32 out of 181—which put me suddenly in the top 18% of my connections.

For the third week, I focused on commenting a lot on articles and updated my status a couple more times again. Those two activities helped me to jump all the way to #17 out of 182 connections.

By week four, I had reached my goal: I was #10 out of 184 connections; in the top 5%! All I had been doing during that time was to continue to "like" and comment on posts. Two weeks later, while continuing this strategy as well as publishing my first long-form post, I ranked #7, in the top 4% of my connections.

Because I was so active on LinkedIn, and because I was ranked high, people began looking at my profile. That was how I was also headhunted by two separate people—one from a fashion store, and the other from a recruiting agency.

The bottom line? Don't neglect LinkedIn if you're looking to make strong business connections!

What I discovered with LinkedIn was that it can be a great way to connect with others if you want to work for a company.

It's not necessarily the most effective tool for freelancers who want to work with small businesses or individuals, *however* if your goal is to have corporate clients, then I believe that LinkedIn is exactly what you'll need to get noticed. Give LinkedIn a try and see if it's right for you!

Settings Your Rates: Some (More) Recommendations

We already discussed this in Chapter 2, but it bears repeating here! Setting rates is something you will constantly have to think about, research, and adjust, from preparing to launch your business to launching your business, to getting new clients, and more.

This is one of the most-debated questions among freelancers: *how much should I charge?*

Unfortunately it's a tough one to answer, because it depends on the type of work you're doing and the rates in your geographical region as well. But overall, I recommend charging about $50 / hour, or about $0.05 / word.

On average, assume that you can write and / or edit approximately 1,000 words in one hour. Depending on the project, it might be closer to 500 words or 2,000 words. But it will likely average out to 1,000 words. Fifty dollars for one hour is very reasonable, and here's why:

You have to keep in mind that as a freelancer, you don't get sick pay, vacation time, benefits, professional development, or an office space provided to you. Instead, you have to pay for all of that yourself. And that means that your hourly rate or project rate is going to be significantly higher than if you worked in a conventional office setting.

Also keep in mind that you will be putting in a lot of unpaid hours, or non-billable hours, every week, between finding clients and marketing your business and dealing with administrative tasks.

As I mentioned earlier in this book, the first time I started freelancing about five years ago, I asked my public relations boss how much he recommend that I charge. He told me to charge no less than $45 / hour. *And that was me starting out as a new freelancer in a city where living costs are relatively low compared to other cities across the country.* I agree with him that around $50 / hour makes the most sense (considering the items I mentioned above), but it is also helpful to **have an internal sliding scale.**

For example, when it comes to a small business that can't afford $50 / hour, but which is a business that I like and I'm rather in need of some employment, I might drop my fees to $25 / hour. Similarly, I have worked at a rate which worked out to $100 / hour for a client that had dollars to spend. Your rate is based partly on the value of your work (and the value of writing and editing really is somewhere in the range of $25 / hour to $100 / hour), and based partly on your client's budget.

Another question that many freelancers ask is whether they should charge by the hour, by the word, or by the project. Ultimately, if you are being fair with your rates, it should work out to roughly the same. Depending on the client and how they want the project to be priced out, I'll quote them any of those. At the rate that I work, $50 / hour and $0.05 / word work out to be approximately the same amount. When it comes to charging your rate by the project (which can be a nice option when you have a strong idea of what the project will involve, since a flat fee is very simple and straightforward to provide a client), you have to estimate how long it will take you to complete the project.

An additional note here: when you are charging by the project (or really, when you are quoting any fees), keep in mind that sometimes projects are slightly trickier than you expected, or that something might come up and hinder you, or that the client might want extra work completed partway through the project. For this reason, **always estimate slightly higher than you expect it to take.** In the end, charge them for the amount that you actually worked, of course—but by estimating slightly higher, you can factor in anything that might come up. And things *will* come up.

If it ends up taking less time than you quoted, and the client has to pay less than they anticipated, they will be very pleased about it, too.

Building Relationships with Current Clients

It's much harder to *find* new clients than to *retain* current ones. So much of being a business owner is really about building and maintaining relationships.

Here are a few key things to keep in mind when you are building relationships with your current clients:

- **Be okay with working intense hours.** Here's the thing with freelancing: you might go for a couple weeks without having any work, and then suddenly three clients will need projects completed within the next two days. This sort of thing happens *all the time.* Your clients care about their businesses as much as you care about yours, and they won't hesitate to email you at 4:00pm asking you to get something on their desk at 9:00am the next day.

Unless you tell all of your clients upfront that you work a set amount of hours, or unless you're willing to lose out on some work, you will need to have to buckle down and be willing to work on evenings and weekends.

A quick note here: I definitely think it's important that clients respect your time, but when you are starting out, sometimes it's better to take that call on Wednesday evening or Sunday morning and get the project turned around *fast* than to refuse to do the work or to have the client think that they can't call you for urgent projects. Over time, as you build long-term relationships with clients, you can start a discussion about how you now only accept work-related calls between certain hours of the day, if you so choose.

- **Go above and beyond.** You don't have to do the bare minimum for your clients, and in fact, you *shouldn't* just do the bare minimum for them. Take an extra hour or two to provide them with an additional service, and they will continue to use your services into the future, provide you with a great testimonial, and share your contact information with their network.

For example, I was hired to write weekly blog posts, monthly e-newsletters, and daily Tweets for a local business. I met with the business owner and he told me what he eventually hoped for on the social media side of things, and I gave him some recommendations and told him my ideas.

Then I ended up taking his basic ideas for things that he wanted "someday" and implemented them into my original ideas, even though he hadn't asked me to do so. He loved it! In addition, I created a social media strategy for his business and presented it to him before I had even got started working on the blog, which he hadn't asked for. He was blown away by the initiative and thoughtfulness I had put into the project.

I share this story with you to illustrate how you can take ideas and run with them. This will set you apart from other freelancers!

- **Connect with your clients as real people.** We talk about relationships with clients because clients aren't just entities with dollar signs for faces—they are real people! Remember that you are dealing with other business owners and people who have ideas and feelings. Get to know them and understand what they want from you and from your business so you can provide them with the services they need, and so you can tailor your work to suit their project. Connect with them in meaningful ways and they will appreciate you that much more.

It depends on the client and the type of work you do, but you can certainly keep connected with clients by adding them on LinkedIn, Twitter, and / or Facebook, or sending them a holiday card in December. These are all good ways to help you to stay top-of-mind for your clients. You can even let clients know that you are available for ongoing work and that you enjoyed working with them and would love to continue working with them in the future. You can even ask them for a testimonial as a way to reconnect after not working with them for a while. Don't be afraid to get creative.

CHAPTER 6: HOW TO SURVIVE & THRIVE WITH THE FREELANCE LIFE

Getting through the first few months can be the toughest part as a new freelancer and home-based business owner! But once you've successfully prepared for and launched your business, and have secured yourself some regular clients, there will be other things you'll have to deal with. The major ones include asking clients for increased rates and testimonials, navigating both busy and quiet times, handling sick days and vacation time, and managing and maintaining your work-life balance. We'll address all of these in this chapter.

Asking to Increase Rates

Okay, this can be an awkward conversation to have—let's just get that out in the open! We all know it's true. But there are a few ways to ensure the conversation takes place organically to make it comfortable for both you and your client, and to increase the chance that your client will agree to an increased rate:

- **Wait until you have been working together for a while.** If you conduct work on a weekly basis, your client is very pleased with the work you have produced, you have provided them with a little extra bang for their buck, and the initial fee is lower than you would like, you can request an increased rate within a few months. If you work with the client a couple times each year, you might want to wait a few years before informing them of your increased rates.

  Note that this also depends on how much you are currently charging. For example, one client pays me approximately $100 /

hour, and so I have no need to request an increase in rates at any time in the near future. However, for my small business clients and clients that I have gotten through Elance, the rates generally start at around $15–$25 / hour. Those are the ones that you definitely want to increase the rates for once you have done some work for these clients and they appreciate and are impressed by the quality of your work.

- **Bring it up at the start of a new project.** Asking midway through a project if the rate can be increased for that project isn't generally appropriate. Wait until you have completed your project and they've asked you to do more work before presenting the idea of increased rates to your client. Discussing it at the beginning of the new project, rather than right at the end of your last project (if there is some time between the two), is also a good idea because it's fresh in both your and your client's minds.

- **Discuss it after your client has expressed their appreciation in your work.** Did you make a small mistake in your last project, such as a typo, which your client noticed and pointed out to you? Now might not be the best time to ask for an increased rate. If your client asks you for more work (and really, most clients will be very forgiving of the rare mistake you make—after all, we're all human!), wait until they have commented on how well you completed the project before you ask for an increased rate on the next project.

  We *are* all human, but at the same time your client is paying for you to produce high-quality work, and you will need to work that much harder to prove yourself if you *do* make a small mistake.

- **Don't ask for an outrageous increase.** Moving from $20 / hour to $25 / hour or from $40 / hour to $50 / hour is perfectly reasonable. Requesting a jump from $20 to $50, or from $40 to $80, is probably going to be a bit much for your clients. Really consider your skills and the services you offer, why it's time for an increased rate (which can be as simple as the cost of living increasing, or that you have achieved some certification in the industry), and what a fair rate would be.

- **Make sure there is a good reason for the increased rate.** It is true that, as mentioned above, you can increase your rates simply because cost of living has increased, but you should consider other factors as well. For example, have you been working with the same client for a few years but when you look back at your original work, it doesn't differ much from the work you produce today? If so, you're going to have a tough time selling the idea of an increased rate.

  You should be able to point out how your work quality has increased or your style has adapted over the years, or at the very least show that you have received a diploma or certification in a new spe-cialization in your industry. The point here is that there should be a *reason* for your rate. Take care to look at this from an impartial per-spective and think about what is a fair rate for all parties involved.

- **Talk about money via email if you're uncomfortable about it.** Talking about fees can feel awkward when you're speaking with a client in person or on the phone. One way to get around this is if your client asks you what a fee will be, you can say that you need to review it and you will email them a proposal. This way, you don't have to provide a number on the spot, and you can ask in a more neutral space (i.e. via email).

  This is an especially good option to go with in case your client asks you to explain your rate. Sometimes it's easier to take the time to write out why your rate is what it is—instead of feeling flustered, turning red, and stumbling over your words as you try to explain it in person. (We all get better at talking about money with time—but for many freelancers, it can take a while.)

How to Ask for an Increased Rate: A Sample Email Response

Hi _____,

Great to hear from you! I'd be happy to work on this project with you—the deadline shouldn't be a problem.

Just a heads up that since we last worked together, I've increased my rates from $50 / hour to $60 / hour after recently completing my Copy Editing Certification with the Editors' Association of Canada. Please let me know if you have any questions about that. Looking forward to working with you again!

Best,
_____.

- **Compromise if necessary.** Did you ask for a $10 / hour raise and your client suggested a $5 / hour raise instead? Unless you can afford to lose the client and their work, I would highly recommend you agree to the negotiated fee. You can always ask for another $5 increase in another six months.

- **Don't be afraid to politely turn down work if the rate is too low.** If you frame your request for increased rates as more of a statement than a question, then you can certainly tell the client that you simply cannot continue working at that rate any longer—as long as you phrase it diplomatically enough, and perhaps even suggest another freelancer who might be willing to complete the work for a rate they feel more comfortable with, it should be fine.

If the rate is really too low for you and you're okay with losing out on some work, then assert yourself! In the event that a client tries to negotiate a rate too low (such as if you ask for a $10 / hour increase and they counter with a $2 / hour increase), be cautious about continuing to work with them. They may not respect you or the work you do.

- **Be gracious if they decline or ask if the increase in rates can wait.** Do you really like this client, enjoy the work, and the increased rate isn't *super* important? If so, graciously accept if a client explains that they can't afford any higher, or if your client asks if the increased rate can begin for the next project instead. These things happen, and are for the most part entirely reasonable.

  On the other hand, if your client is a bully and you don't enjoy working with them, now would be a good time to graciously bow out and explain that you can't continue to work for them at that rate any longer.

- **Consider each client before making the request.** Some clients have larger budgets than others. Some might send a lot of work your way. Some might be friends of yours. There are a lot of things to consider when it comes to asking for increased rates, and it is okay to keep your rates the same for some people and request increases from others if there are special cases.

  For example, there is one woman for whom I will likely never change my rate because even though I should probably be making double the amount that I'm currently making, she's worked with me right from the beginning, she's a family friend, and the rate isn't completely ridiculous. I'm okay with working for her at a cheaper rate than for others. Another option that you could consider, if your rates are the same for all of your current clients, is to only raise the rates for new clients, at least in the beginning.

Requesting Testimonials from Clients

Testimonials, references, and recommendations can be a great way to illustrate your talents and skills. It's one thing for *you* to say that you are great with deadlines and extremely detail-oriented—but it's a whole other thing for one of your *clients* to rave about you and say the same thing. Testimonials can make a huge difference for whether or not you get new clients. Include the testimonials as a separate, easy-to-find page on your website so they are more easily accessible.

Just as with requesting for a rate increase, sometimes it can feel awkward to approach clients about providing you with testimonials. Here's how you can make the request for testimonials from your clients (and actually *get* the testimonials, too):

- **Send the request to your top clients.** By all means, do *not* request a testimonial from anyone with whom you didn't get along, only did one project for five years ago, or whose project you made even the smallest mistake on (unless that was a long time ago and they were very gracious about it). Request testimonials from clients you have worked with for a long time and who regularly express their appreciation for your work. Ask for testimonials from the clients that you have gone above and beyond for.

  One freelancer friend includes an invitation for clients to give feedback at the bottom of each invoice. That's certainly another (more passive) way to connect with clients you have yet to build a relationship with but would still like a testimonial from.

- **Let them know what you want from them.** Explain in your request why you are asking for a testimonial, and give as much detail as possible about what you are hoping to get from them. If you want testimonials about your skillset, your work ethic, or your work style, *let your clients know that.* They will be happy to tailor their testimonial so it reflects their feelings and opinions about you and your work, while going at it from the angle that is of the most benefit to you.

Be very clear about what you are asking for and how much you are asking from them, too. Even a sentence or two can be effective. Let your clients know that so it doesn't seem like a huge amount of "work" for them. If you can point them to your testimonials page with examples already on it, that would be even better so they can get a feel for what you're after.

- **Be considerate of your clients.** Remember that this is a request, not a demand! While you are giving them specific details, also be sure to note that there is no pressure. Unless you really need those testimonials by a specific deadline, don't request that they send you a testimonial within a certain timeframe—use phrases such as "at your leisure" or "when you get the chance."

Be sure to let your clients know that you can proofread the testimonial for them before posting it on your website. This is about making things *as simple and easy as possible for your clients*. If they ask you to write the testimonial for them and then run it by them before publishing it, then by all means do that. But otherwise, I wouldn't offer to write it for them—ultimately it's much better to have it in their words.

- **Thank them.** It is courteous to send an appreciative response once you get that testimonial. Be sure to let them know that you are grateful for the time they put in to provide you with a thoughtful testimonial that you can publish on your website.

How to Navigate Really Busy Times

Just so we're clear, *busy* means *good* for freelancers! But it can also be a challenge to juggle everything. Here are some tips for navigating those really busy times:

- **Breathe.** First things first: calm down and try not to get overwhelmed or stressed out. The situation probably isn't as scary as you think. Engage in some relaxation techniques if you are feeling too over-whelmed before you actually get started working on the projects.

- **Prioritize and estimate the amount of time each project will take.** What needs to be completed first? How many hours will it all take you? Once you've made your estimates, is it realistic to finish every-thing by your deadlines? Often if you separate your projects and calculate the rough amounts of time each project will take, you'll find you can easily complete all of it on time.

  Quick note here: you should *always* ask clients for deadlines or approximate timeframes for submitting the completed project. Be sure that both you and your client are aware of how important the project is and when it needs to be returned by.

- **Let things go that aren't priorities.** When things get really busy for me, that's when I set personal projects aside and don't put as much effort into marketing my business. The important thing to do is to get the job completed on time, and to provide a really high-quality finished product.

- **Remove distractions and set up rewards.** Shut down Facebook and Twitter. Tell yourself that you can go out with friends for drinks at the end of the day *only* if you first finish XYZ with your projects. Get rid of anything that will distract you: just focus on work. If you know you have something to look forward to once you have completed the work, you will also be more motivated.

On the other hand, if you feel like you are experiencing burnout and you are having a tough time pushing through and finishing the project, it might be best to take a walk or get away from the computer for an hour or two. This can be a great way to feel refreshed and re-energized! The important thing is to *be honest* with yourself about whether you need a break or if you just need to push yourself harder.

- **Remember that it's not always going to be like this.** Enjoy the really busy times, because you will be wishing for them when business slows down! You might feel a little tired now, but you'll have a break soon enough. It seems to be a rule that freelance work comes in peaks and troughs, and it's something you will get used to with time.

What to Do When Business Slows Down

Here we have the other side of the coin: you get a little break from the intensity of all that work, but you have to deal with the nagging anxiety about where your next job will come from. Rather than worry about it, why not *do* something about it?

Here are some excellent ways to make great use of your time when business slows down:

- **Engage in some professional development and / or take the time to do research on your industry.** When things get busy, we tend not to do as much research into our industry, but it's very important to be in the know and keep up to speed. When business slows down, you have yourself an excellent opportunity to do that research! This is also a good time to take an online course and brush up on your skills, attend a webinar, or go to a workshop related to business or your industry.

- **Deal with administrative tasks.** The administration component of your business may fall by the wayside during busy times. Catch up on those things now, while you can! You will feel great about having tackled administrative tasks, and those are probably very important items that you needed to cross off your list anyway.

- **Build relationships and find new clients.** Check in with your current clients: send them an email to say hello, connect with them on social media, or meet them for coffee. Also take this opportunity to market and promote your business to try to find new clients. Spend that time on social media to build your networks, attending events where you can meet potential clients, and putting together your new flyers or business cards.

- **Request testimonials.** This is a nice way to a) build your business and showcase your talents, and b) remind your clients that you are around! If you reconnect with past clients and you have a *reason* for connecting with them—such as requesting a testimonial—it will be a good reminder for them about you and your work, and it might just give them the boost they need to offer you more work.

- **Take care of your personal life.** You might have neglected friends and family or your own health and wellbeing when things were really busy. Take this time to socialize, spring-clean your home, go for long walks, and cook healthy meals. Engage in activities you enjoy; relax and have a good time. This will reenergize you for when work starts coming in again.

- **Work on a personal business-related project.** There are always little personal projects related to your work that you can spend your time on. Whether it's putting together a collection of your writing samples, revamping your business website, working on a book about your industry, or planning a training workshop, there are bound to be lots of things you always *want* to work on but never seem to have the time or energy for. Now is the time to engage in those projects (case in point: I wrote the first draft of this book during a slower business time).

Sick Days and Vacation: How Does It Work?

When you're a freelancer, you don't necessarily get a set amount of sick days each year. You can't wake up in the morning and call your boss to let them know you're not coming in to work. No one else can cover for you when you're sick.

Sick days are tricky to manage. If you spend most of your time at home, your immune system might not be as strong as it used to be. For example, one of my freelancing gigs includes transcribing university lectures for deaf and hard-of-hearing students. That means that when school starts in September, I'm exposed to *tons* of germs at the university, being in small classrooms full of students. I always get a bad cold and sore throat by the middle of the month, and it makes it frustrating to do work when I just want to curl up on the couch with a big bowl of soup.

One of the ways you can combat this is to try to get work done well before deadlines. If you are always a couple days ahead, *it won't be such a big deal to take a day or two off.* However, if you aren't in the position of being ahead of schedule, it's best to contact your clients as soon as possible to let them know you're feeling under the weather and you need an extension on deadlines. In this scenario, focus on getting the priority items completed first. When you're sick, you only have the energy to do so many things—so make it count!

I have never been so ill that I couldn't check my emails, so I don't use an autoresponder letting people know that I'll be away from the computer. Instead, when I'm ill, I check my email a couple times each day and stay in contact with clients as I normally would. If any new projects come my way,

I explain that I'm not feeling well and that I'll be able to get to their project in a few days when I'm feeling better.

Vacation days are a little different than sick days. If you take a vacation, try to actually take that vacation! Plan ahead as much as you can, and let your long-term clients know in advance that you'll be going away. Put together a plan for what will happen while you're gone, too. When I travelled for several weeks one summer, I contacted a few clients six weeks before I actually left. These were clients that I managed social media for, so it was important they were aware that I would be away. When I told them my vacation dates, I also assured them that I would schedule all social media posts in advance—and I explained explicitly which dates I would be completely out of contact.

What about legislated holidays and long weekends? Think long and hard about what these mean for you and your business. Who are your clients? One of the best parts about freelancing is that you can work for people all over the world—but that also means that different people have different types of important holidays. My clients are mostly based in Canada and the United States, but even then I have to navigate Canada Day and Independence Day, as well as our different Thanksgiving Days, for example. American clients will contact me for rush jobs on July 1st, just the same way that Canadian clients will contact me for rush jobs on July 4th. Because of that, I don't tend to take many of these types of holidays completely off—I usually make a point of checking my email a couple times a day if I will be celebrating the holiday myself; otherwise, I just treat it like a regular work day.

Regardless of whether you are taking the day off to celebrate a legislated holiday or if you are leaving town for a two-week vacation, it's very important to have a vacation responder in place on your email (and also your voicemail, if clients contact you primarily over the phone) so clients are aware that you're away or unavailable and won't be getting back to them until a specific date.

When it comes to how much vacation time you should take each year, it's completely a personal preference—and it depends how much time you can afford to take away from your business.

I like to take "working holidays," where I have access to the Internet and I'm still available to answer client questions at least once a day via email. For the first couple of years as a full-time freelancer, I recommend taking no more than two to three weeks of vacation time (and no more than one full week of that without access to Internet). Do as much work as you can before going on vacation so you don't have to worry too much about it while you're on holiday—but at the same time, remember that a perfect job for you could come up while you're away. You wouldn't want to miss out on that, would you?

Choose your vacation time wisely, and realize that you probably won't be able to take a "real" vacation, Internet-free, for very long periods of time during your first few years as a new business owner. But if you play your cards right, you could set yourself up to take regular month-long vacations after you've established yourself.

How to Manage and Maintain Your Work-Life Balance

As a freelancer and a home-based business owner, you will think about your business all the time. This isn't just a necessity—it's also simply what will happen, whether you like it or not.

My mother, a small business owner herself, often comments that "no one will care about your business as much as you do." This is very true. Your family members, your clients, even your employees or co-workers, if you have them, simply will not care about and think about your business as much as you do. And that's okay! But it's a good reminder that if you don't put in the time and the effort for your business, no one will. If you can't make your business work, no one can.

I think about my business when I wake up in the morning. I think about my business when I am conducting business activities. I think about my business when I'm taking breaks and enjoying my personal life. I think about my business when I go to sleep at night. But that's not necessarily a bad thing, and here's why: **when you are your brand, it doesn't feel like such a big deal to think about work and business all the time.**

Having a healthy work-life balance is very important. Having some boundaries between work and play is also important. But when your work and your personal life mesh, you don't have to worry so much about maintaining boundaries and separating the two. As a home-based business owner, you have the luxury of overlapping your work with your play *all the time.*

This is good for your business, because it means you are constantly promoting and marketing yourself in everything that you do when you *are* your brand. This is also good for your personal life, because it means that even when you are working, you are probably still enjoying it immensely and getting a lot out of it.

The one piece of advice that I will give here, as we reach the end of this chapter and near the end of the book, is this: **listen to your body.** If you start feeling tired, if you are starting to drag your feet, if you aren't excited about working, if you make a mistake or two, if you aren't being as productive as usual, or if your work is coming along very slowly, *those are all signs that you need to take a break!*

I don't personally plan for time off from work, as a general rule: instead, I work every day of the week. But when I notice any of those things happening, I'll take a day or three off, or I'll work a half-day instead of a full day. By giving yourself a little rest, you'll maintain good work-life balance, and you will be that much more ready to jump into things again after the break.

CHAPTER 7: FREQUENTLY ASKED QUESTIONS ABOUT BUSINESS, WRITING, & EDITING

Before our eighth and final chapter of this book, let's go through a few of the most common questions that come up with new freelancers / business owners. These are some of the big questions I've received from friends and acquaintances who are thinking about starting their own freelancing business, so I wanted to set them all aside here towards the end of the book so you can have easy access to the answers!

1. How do I become a freelancer?

Hopefully you will already have the answer to this from reading the rest of this book! But in a nutshell, you become a freelancer by registering your business (as I mentioned earlier, talk to an accountant to find out how to go about doing that), getting the skills you need in your field, finding clients, and producing high-quality, timely work.

Anyone can become a freelancer! The trick is to have the right personality traits (besides the business smarts and work skills) to be successful at freelancing.

2. ...Okay, so what are the key personality traits to being a successful freelancer?

I'm glad you asked!

In general, you know you're cut out to be a freelancer if you are...

- Disciplined (you'll need to be your own boss, after all).

- Good at wearing many hats (you'll have to be your own boss, employee, office manager, and secretary, at the very least!).

- Comfortable working (and being) alone for long periods of time.

- Independent.

- A critical thinker.

- Creative.

- Confident (and believe in yourself).

- Resilient (you're going to have to pick yourself up again when—not if—you fail or get rejected).

Some of these skills can be developed over time. Many of us won't really know just how good we'll be at freelancing until we try it, either.

3. If I don't have ANY experience, what do I do about my portfolio?

If you don't have any experience at all, keep in mind that we *all* start at the beginning. You're not alone!

This can be tricky, of course: clients want to see work you've done for other clients before they hire you, but they need to hire you before you can have work to show in your portfolio. So when you're first starting out, I recommend beginning by doing volunteer work, or helping a friend or family member with a small project.

For example, you could offer to edit a professional letter your friend is writing, and then use Track Changes to show what you added (of course, you'll want to block out some words / phrases for privacy purposes if you use this as a public portfolio item).

There are so many non-profits that are in desperate need of volunteer work—you could write copy for posters, help out with the blog, write social media posts or press releases, or edit their newsletter articles, for example. Get creative!

4. Where can I find work?

A better question might be, where *can't* you find work? There is work to be had everywhere!

However, you will most likely find that the best places to find work as a freelancer in the beginning are online freelancing sites, through word of mouth (make sure your family, friends, and past clients are passing your business cards along!), and Google. When your website is optimized for search engines, contains great content, and is well-marketed on social media, clients begin coming to you.

Think about who your ideal client is and where they would spend their time. Then go to the places they frequent and start networking.

5. Should I take every project I can get? How do I know when to say "yes" or "no" to a new client / project?

This is a complex issue that every freelancer faces. Unfortunately, it boils down to how much work you personally can take on and

fit into a day or a week... as well as what your personality is like.

I strongly encourage new freelancers to take pretty much all the work they can get in the first three to six months. That might mean doing some work that doesn't really interest you, working for a ridiculously small fee, and having clients that you just don't "click" with.

While I certainly don't think you should say "yes" to absolutely everything for the rest of your freelancing career, *in the beginning, you just have to say "yes" a lot.*

Think about it this way: if you don't have any experience, how are you going to get better at what you do? If you don't have any portfolio items, how can you show new clients what you're capable of? If you aren't making money (no matter how little some clients might pay you), how are you going to pay the bills?

The key is to always look for more clients and more projects. You might be able to be choosy about projects within just a few months of freelancing... or it could take you a few years.

After freelancing full-time for a year and a half, I am just getting to the point where I know that I can theoretically say "no" to potential clients, because I'm getting enough work and making enough money per project to sustain myself. But keep in mind that when you say "no" to a client, they might never come back to you again. Just because you're busy now doesn't mean that you'll be busy three weeks from now. Will you regret saying "no" if things change over the next few weeks?

Freelancing is a constant balance of getting enough work and not getting burned out—and only you can know what that means to you. When it doubt, say "yes" to more work and set the deadline for significantly longer than you think it will take you to complete the project, just in case you get too frazzled or burned out with your workload. As a freelancer, it's best to default to "yes" rather than "no."

6. How do you spend your days? What kinds of hours should I be keeping as a freelancer?

I've provided two examples of what my day has looked like, hour by hour, in Appendix IV—so I encourage you look there to see an idea of what this freelancer's day looks like.

The hours that you keep depends on your business, your work style, and your lifestyle. However, in general, I recommend starting your work day earlier in the morning, if possible, and squeezing in some hours in the evenings and on weekends when they allow for it.

Be mindful of working in a schedule that's right for you: if that means sleeping in until 11am and getting your best work done at 2am, then by all means, go for it. On the other hand, if you have small children at home, you might find that your workday will be broken up based on when your kids are napping or at daycare, for example.

Keep in mind that for the first year, at least, you should be prepared to work some, if not most, evenings and weekends. You won't see results if you don't put in the work to make it happen. There is no right or wrong way to do freelancing, but if you find yourself feeling exhausted and you have too much work to do, then maybe you should cut back on your hours. On the other hand, if you feel energized and you haven't had any client work in days, maybe you should hustle a little more and put the extra hours in.

7. I'm pretty good at writing... so I can probably just become a freelancer in a couple weeks once I've given my notice at my day job, right?

Probably NOT, actually.

Being good at whatever it is you want to do as a freelancer—be it writing, editing, graphic design, web development, etc.—is only one half of the freelancing coin. The other side of it is that you need to be good at business if you really want to succeed. That means being disciplined, hustling to find clients, and working long hours, for a start.

You will also want to take some time to prepare yourself for becoming a freelancer (refer back to Chapters 2—4 if you need a refresher!) before you simply quit your regular job, especially if you don't have any clients or business experience. Be as prepared as you can so that you truly set yourself up for success.

I recommend working on the sidelines to build up your portfolio, client list, and savings, for at the very least a couple of months, before taking the plunge and becoming a full-time freelancer.

8. Do I need to put together a contract for clients?

A contract is always a good idea!

At the minimum, simply having a record of an email correspondence that confirms the parameters of the project, the fee, and the deadline is certainly better than nothing, but a contract lends a little more professionalism and legitimacy to your business and your work. I have provided a sample contract template in Appendix VII in this book, which you can certainly take and modify to your liking (you can also find contract templates through most national freelancing organization websites).

Contracts may seem stiff and formal, but they are useful reference documents and help to protect both you *and* your client. Get as much as you can in writing—avoid relying on verbal agreements as that could cause serious problems for you down the line.

9. How soon can I expect to start to make "real" money and support myself?

This depends on how much you put into your business, how much you charge, the types of clients you have, the amount you need to support yourself, etc.

However, as a general rule, expect to have some lean times in the beginning. Assuming you take the time to network and find work, you can expect to make a decent amount within six months of starting to freelance full-time, and you should certainly be making enough money to support yourself within the first year.

Your income will likely fluctuate a fair amount from month to month, so don't be surprised if it takes a while before your income starts to come in more steadily.

10. Working from home is too distracting for me. What are my other options?

If you have small kids at home or if you just want a space away from the house to work, you can certainly work out of coffee shops or the library some days of the week. This is also a nice way to get out and interact with other people for a while (something which you might be missing out on by working by yourself all the time).

Another great option is a shared office space with other free-lancers. As the number of people freelancing has increased over the years, offices for freelancers have become a popular option. Research your city to find out if there are offices to rent near you— they are often small spaces that share the same floor so you'll be around other freelancers, and most of them are fairly reasonably priced. Renting one of these offices can also help you feel more like you're "going to work" each day if you have a tough time focusing on work at home.

11. How much education or experience do I need before I can call myself a writer and / or editor? What kind of certification / courses / diploma / degree do I need? What courses / training can (or should!) I take to improve my skills?

If you have a natural talent for writing, you can technically become a professional writer with little formal training. Just remember that the more you practice and the more you learn from others, the better you'll continue to get!

It's important to be honest with yourself about how good your writing skills are: don't let your ego get the best of you. Find your voice and you will be a better writer for it. Then, you can brush up on your skills through taking a writing class, or even diving right into the job market by bidding on gigs through a freelancing job site or building up your portfolio by doing volunteer work, such as writing for the local community newspaper.

Becoming a professional editor is a little different than becoming a professional writer, however, because you *do* need professional training to be an editor. National editing bodies, such as the Editors' Association of Canada and the (American) Editorial Freelancers

Association, often have certification programs and / or workshops for members.

You can even get a degree in publishing or communications at a number of different universities, or you can audit university classes related to your field if money is especially tight: be sure to be honest with your clients that you don't have a degree in publishing, but that you have sat in on the classes and done all of the materials for these classes. Some universities like MIT even have all of their course material available online for free, which is another good option for brushing up on your skills at your own pace without blowing your budget.

No two writers or editors will become a writer or editor the same way. There isn't one particular course or degree you should absolutely get if you want to make it in this field, but keep in mind that it's smart to always do more training, no matter how much background and experience you have in the field. And if you're having a tough time getting clients, that might be a sign that you need more formal training, education, or experience so clients see you as being more credible or legitimate.

There's always more to learn! Your work will be the better for it if you brush up on your skills regularly, too.

12. What background documents or materials should I prepare for meeting with potential clients?

There are all kinds of different materials you might want to provide

to potential clients. Different clients will have different requests of you; get as much ready as possible so you're well-prepared.

Some materials you might want to have ready to provide your client with include your resume, a couple testimonials of your work (you can direct the client to your website for that information), and your portfolio or a few pieces of past work that you've done.

In addition, prepare rates ahead of time. As much as possible, I try not to give clients a number the first time we're discussing the project because it can be better to mull it over and weigh how much this project is really worth, especially if you are doing a project-based fee (when you're put on the spot at an in-person meeting, you run the risk of drastically over- or under-estimating the amount of time and work involved).

However, you should at the very least be able to provide an estimate or a range at the time of your meeting in case they press for hard numbers. You can also offer the client information on specific services or packages that you do (for example, if you want to "bundle" services together at a slightly reduced rate).

Lastly, bring along a notebook and pen so you can take notes. And write down any questions you have for the client ahead of time! If you are meeting them in person, you won't want to forget any important questions to ask. Some of your questions may include things like:

- What is your deadline for this project?
- What is your vision or ultimate goal with this project?
- You said you want a copy editor—can you outline in more detail what you're looking for in an editor? (This is an important question to ask, because many clients won't understand the different between a proofreader and a copy editor, or a copy editor and a stylistic editor, for example. They might say they want a copy editor when

they really need a developmental editor. It's best to identify that as soon as possible!)

- My typical rate is somewhere around ____. What's your budget like?
- What are your expectations for this project?

After the client answers each of these questions, you might want to repeat what they said back to them to confirm that you understood them correctly.

13. My client wants me to sign a Non-Disclosure Agreement – should I do that?

This isn't an uncommon practice. If you are editing a manuscript, the author might be very protective of their work and concerned about someone stealing their idea or sharing their idea with other people before their book has been published. Non-Disclosure Agreements (NDAs) are just fine to sign.

Be sure to always read everything thoroughly, and remember that you can ask your client questions if you have concerns about the agreement, or you can get someone with a legal background to check it over for you before you sign it.

14. Do I NEED to have a blog if I'm a freelancer?

You absolutely need to have a website as a freelancer—you need a place you can direct people to which is your own platform (i.e. not LinkedIn or Facebook).

Should a blog be part of that website? I'm hesitant to say that every freelancer should have a blog, partly because it might depend on you and your business, and partly because blogging, like any form of social media, can take up a great deal of time—and just like any other type of social media outlet, it's better to not have a blog than to blog poorly or inconsistently.

However, as a freelance writer, your blog can be the number one place where potential clients can see your voice, writing style, and skill. Even blogging once or twice a month will be worth something! Editors can get away without having a blog, however blogs are a great way to keep people coming back to your website... and it could transform everyday readers into clients, too.

Don't rush into this decision. Think through it carefully to decide if a blog is right for you and your brand, and then take the time to brainstorm ideas and schedule articles in advance. This is also why I recommend getting a Wordpress.org website; you can easily use it as a static website or as a blog. It's very user-friendly in that way.

The types of things you can blog about vary drastically, of course, but if you want to use it as a marketing tool for your business, you can blog about everything from your experiences of becoming a freelancer to writing / editing tips to an ongoing fiction story and more. The options are endless!

CHAPTER 8: CAUTION! THINGS TO WATCH OUT FOR AS A FREELANCER

At some point or another, you might run into any of these situations! Here's how to watch out for and deal with them:

- **People who want you to work for free or work for an amount that is less than what you're worth.** While I highly recommend having a couple volunteering gigs going, don't just jump into the first thing that someone wants you to do. I've made this mistake once or twice and I ended up doing a mediocre job because I just wasn't really interested in the organization or the work.

  Instead, think about which organizations you would like to volunteer for, and what type of work you would like to do, and approach them. When people approach you out of the blue asking you to volunteer for them, especially if it's an organization you know little about or aren't interested in, politely decline. That's a huge red flag, to have a stranger ask you to do pro bono work!

  Another problem you'll run into is people who want to pay you significantly less than you're worth. As we've discussed in this book, you might want to make allowances for some situations (such as if you get along with the client really well). For other occasions, however, just say "no." It's your business, and you get to call the shots. Politely explain why your fees are what they are, and if they still want to pay you a fifth of what you're worth, you can just walk away. It's not worth it.

What about if friends or family ask you to do work for them? Be careful about this! Never say "yes" immediately. Take the time to ask them questions about what is involved with the work they want you to do. Will it take up hours upon hours of your time? Is it work you're interested in? What will you get out of it?

There have been plenty of times when I've happily given my time and knowledge for free. There have also been other times when I've explained that I don't have the time to do XYZ. One good friend of mine, another freelancer, happens to have skills in an area that I do not (namely, web design and graphic design), and I was willing to pay for his work, but he suggested we swap skills instead. That ended up helping me immensely because the work he did would have cost me thousands of dollars, and I've also been able to provide him with writing copy, editing work, business advice, and even nutrition consulting—without any financial issues coming between us.

In the end, there's a big difference between the stranger who wants you to do 30 hours of pro bono work for a non-profit you've never heard of, compared to a friend who could use some of your skills. Learn the difference and remember that no two strangers or friends are alike – think carefully before doing any kind of work for free!

- **Getting hired to do work that isn't quite what you *want* to do, but it pays the bills.** This is such a tricky one. On the one hand, I'm a big proponent of *take whatever work you can get!* On the other hand, you really need to be careful not to spend too much time doing work outside of your field or interest.

The best thing you can do is to accept some of the work, but leave a certain number of hours open each week to spend your time trying to find the work you *actually* want to be doing. And if you're offered gigs that want to pay you $10 / hour to do something you despise, don't be afraid to walk away. If you are in desperate need of money, then this might be exactly the push you need to get hustling.

- **Navigating friends and family who think that you working from home doesn't *really* count as working.** You may have people ask you to run errands for them, or people might make condescending remarks about how you're unemployed, and so on. Keep in mind that *only you know how hard you are working.*

If your spouse has never worked from home before, you will also want to make sure to have multiple conversations about your work with them before and during your freelancing experience. Just because you work from home, doesn't mean that your work is any less important than theirs. And while I personally love to clean my home when I need a break from my work, that might not be your style—and your spouse shouldn't expect to come home to a clean house and dinner on the table just because you've been at home all day.

Try not to take it personally when people assume you're not working, or when they assume that you're only freelancing because you couldn't get hired anywhere else. *You* know that this is a life choice that is right for you, and *you* know that you are working hard. Educate them little by little over time, or let it go!

- **Clients who don't respect personal boundaries.** One of my clients prefers to text as a way to communicate with me. To be honest, I *hate* texting about work matters. Another client has posted on my personal Facebook wall numerous times with things that might be useful for a project I worked on—which isn't exactly ideal, since it's *my* personal Facebook wall.

The thing is that I truly like both of those clients, and so I let it go. I dealt with it by making a point of sliding a subtle comment several times into conversation about how the best way to reach me is email, and that has helped these clients to use email instead of texting or Facebook as a means of contacting me.

Another client called me in the evening once to edit a project that he needed done in a couple of hours. We had only worked together once before, and he wasn't exactly a warm person. I dealt with the project and haven't worked with him since.

You will always have clients who feel like they can call you up at a moment's notice, any time of the day or night, and seemingly assume that you are just sitting around waiting for them to call. You can handle this in a few ways: first, you can make it a rule to never give anyone your phone number; second, you can gently (or subtly) explain that the best way to contact you is XYZ; third, you can tell your clients that you need at least X hours of notice before working on a project or that you only work regular office hours; fourth, you can just suck it up.

While I do give my phone number to clients, it's not something I give out right away. I'll wait for the client to specifically request my phone number. You can do this and take it a step further by explaining that they should only use your phone number for emergencies, and otherwise it's best to reach you via email.

Regardless, if it becomes a problem where a client is routinely interfering with your personal life, it might be time to have a polite, friendly chat about boundaries.

- **Neglecting your health and wellness.** You weren't expecting this one, were you?!

When I first started freelancing full-time, I thought for sure that I would have no problem going to the gym every day and eat super healthy. I was going to finally lose 20 pounds and be in perfect shape!

...Instead, I found myself exercising less and resorting to snack food more and more. In fact, it took me a good year to really find my rhythm to eat well, exercise regularly, and take some much-needed time for self-care (and it's something I'm still working on!).

Having both a standing desk and a regular sitting desk can be an effective way to get you on your feet for part of the day. You can even construct a makeshift standing desk by placing your laptop on a large, sturdy box on your desk and setting your laptop on it. Take the time to roll your shoulders back regularly throughout the day; touch your toes and reach up to the sky. Set a timer every 15–30 minutes to remind yourself to stretch if you have trouble with it. Set up a mirror alongside your desk so you can glance in it and check your posture regularly, too. And always have a tall glass of water within arm's reach.

Make fitness a priority in your life. Start your day with a healthy, balanced breakfast. Do some meditation, yoga, or have quiet time every day. Get outside for fresh air and to stretch your legs. I promise you that taking the time away from your business will actually *benefit* your business: you will have more energy, and the time away from your computer will give you an opportunity to daydream and come up with new and creative ideas for your business. Win-win!

Now That You Are a Pro Freelancer...

Congratulations—you made it to the end of the book! But what's this? There are still quite a few pages left!

The next section of this book is full of all the templates you need to get your business really rolling. From samples of what a day in the life of a freelancer is like, to a template of a business plan, to daily checklists and spreadsheets you can customize to fit your lifestyle, the appendices in this book are the tools you need to take your business off the paper from the theoretical to the practical.

I hope this book provides you with the tools and templates you need to create the foundation of your business. We packed a lot of information into these eight chapters (and into the following eight appendices!), so I encourage you to go back through and reread the book several times. Print this book out, highlight sections that you want to come back to, and jot notes in the margins.

You will constantly learn new things as a freelancer. I'm still learning new things every day (and I love that!). If you want to get more resources, tips, and ideas for being a freelancer, starting your small business, and getting organized and productive, feel free to visit the Writing & Business section of my website (SaganMorrow.com) to find out what new things I've learned and am sharing with YOU even after this book is published. That section of my blog is updated every Wednesday with new articles.

If you have more questions, please don't hesitate to contact me at sagan. morrow@gmail.com, or connect with me on social media. I'm so excited for you to begin your freelancing journey—you're going to rock it!

APPENDIX I: FIVE STEPS TO BETTER PROOFREADING

Use this cheat sheet to ensure that your writing is free from small errors and mistakes. Ask yourself these questions before sharing your writing with the world.

Have I...

1. **Read over my document in its entirety?**

   ☐ Read through the entire document.

   ☐ Complete any unfinished sentences and add content where necessary.

   ☐ Use some kind of Spell Check program to eliminate obvious errors.

2. **Checked that my punctuation is correct?**

   ☐ Complete each sentence with some form of punctuation.

   ☐ Ensure all punctuation is used correctly (such as semi-colons).

   ☐ Place apostrophes in the correct spots.

   ☐ Complete question-framed sentences with a question mark.

3. **Reviewed my grammar and sentence structure?**

   ☐ Double-check words with tricky spellings (such as *their*, *they're*, and *there*).

☐ Use capital letters at the start of every sentence.

☐ Review for any typos or spelling mistakes.

☐ Ensure sentences and phrases are clear and coherent.

4. Checked for consistency?

☐ Check that the same tense is used throughout the entire piece.

☐ Double-check the formatting of the document.

☐ Ensure that the content itself is consistent.

5. Completed a second read-through of the document?

☐ Read it out loud to ensure the content makes sense.

☐ Check that sentences aren't too long and / or complicated.

☐ Ask someone else to read the document to ensure the content is clear.

APPENDIX II: THE ONLY BLOG CHECKLIST YOU'LL EVER NEED

Use this cheat sheet to ensure that your writing is clean, your blog is appealing, and you market yourself right. Ask yourself these questions before publishing your blog posts.

Have I...

1. **Crafted my blog post as a story?**

   ☐ Use a captivating headline which can draw the reader in (hint: think about the headlines YOU like, and draw your inspiration from them!).

   ☐ Give your blog post a story arc—even if it's a list-style blog post, it should still contain a beginning, middle, and an end.

   ☐ Complete any unfinished sentences and add content where necessary.

2. **Checked my writing style and grammar?**

   ☐ Double-check words with tricky spellings (such as *their, they're,* and *there*).

   ☐ Ensure all punctuation is used correctly (such as semi-colons).

   ☐ Place apostrophes in the correct spots.

   ☐ Review for any typos or spelling mistakes.

   ☐ Ensure sentences and phrases are clear and coherent.

3. **Considered the visual appeal?**

    ☐ Add relevant photos, images, and graphics; include captions where appropriate.

    ☐ Add headings to break up the content of your blogs posts.

    ☐ Use bullet points, steps, and color to add some extra flair.

4. **Planned for the marketing component?**

    ☐ Add relevant links to other blog posts on your website or to relevant pages on external websites.

    ☐ Include an appropriate "call to action" at the end of your blog post (ask a question, invite readers to visit another website, etc.).

    ☐ Publish your link to social media sites using appropriate hashtags.

APPENDIX III: SAMPLE BUSINESS PLAN TEMPLATE

{Business Name} Business Plan

{Industry or Field}

{Mission statement}

Business Goals

1. {Specific, measurable, attainable, realistic, and timely goal #1}
2. {Specific, measurable, attainable, realistic, and timely goal #2}
3. {Specific, measurable, attainable, realistic, and timely goal #3}

My five-year vision for my business: {vision statement}.

Target Audiences

Three types of people who will benefit the most from my services / products are:

1. {Target audience #1}
2. {Target audience #2}
3. {Target audience #3}

My ideal client would be: {ideal client description}.

Marketing Strategy

The main social media platform my clients use is {platform name}.

The main geographic location where my clients are located is {geographical location}.

The types of environments, events, and / or businesses that my clients spend their time is {description of type of event or business locale}.

Based on these contributing factors and the above demographics of my target audience, the top three ways to market them (such as flyers, connecting with them via social media, and attending networking events) include:

1. {Marketing strategy #1}
2. {Marketing strategy #2}
3. {Marketing strategy #3}

I will spend approximately {number} hours each week on marketing and promoting my business. Broken down, this will amount to:

*   {Number} hours on {marketing strategy #1}.
*   {Number} hours on {marketing strategy #2}.
*   {Number} hours on {marketing strategy #3}.

Work Plan

TIME OF DAY	WEEKDAY ACTIVITIES	WEEKEND ACTIVITIES
6am	{Activity / task}	{Activity / task}
8am	{Activity / task}	{Activity / task}
10am	{Activity / task}	{Activity / task}
12pm	{Activity / task}	{Activity / task}
2pm	{Activity / task}	{Activity / task}
4pm	{Activity / task}	{Activity / task}
6pm	{Activity / task}	{Activity / task}

Budget

I am allowing 15% of my income to go towards professional development, business expenses, and other freelancing supports. My estimated income for the year is {amount in dollars}, and 15% of that is {amount in dollars}.

ITEM	ESTIMATED COST
{Item}	{Amount}
{Item}	{Amount}
{Item}	{Amount}
{Item}	{Amount}
{Item}	{Amount}
{Item}	{Amount}
TOTAL	{Total cost, approximately equal to 15% of total yearly income}

Financial Goals

MONTH	ESTIMATED TYPE OF PROJECT / AMOUNT OF WORK	ESTIMATED INCOME
January	{Type of project and / or amount of work expected}	{Amount}
February	{Type of project and / or amount of work expected}	{Amount}
March	{Type of project and / or amount of work expected}	{Amount}
April	{Type of project and / or amount of work expected}	{Amount}
May	{Type of project and / or amount of work expected}	{Amount}
June	{Type of project and / or amount of work expected}	{Amount}
July	{Type of project and / or amount of work expected}	{Amount}
August	{Type of project and / or amount of work expected}	{Amount}
September	{Type of project and / or amount of work expected}	{Amount}
October	{Type of project and / or amount of work expected}	{Amount}
November	{Type of project and / or amount of work expected}	{Amount}
December	{Type of project and / or amount of work expected}	{Amount}
TOTAL		{Total income}

APPENDIX IV: SAMPLE OF A DAY IN THE LIFE OF A FREELANCER

This is what a typical day looked like for me when I first started freelancing:

6:30am Wake up, spend 30 minutes running outdoors or practicing yoga indoors, and then clean up and get ready for the day.

8am Have coffee and enjoy breakfast at my computer while I check emails and update social media (for me, that's LinkedIn, Twitter, Facebook, Pinterest, and Instagram).

9:30am Work on a project for a client.

1pm Eat some lunch and take a break to get outside or read a book.

2:30pm Do some research on my industry, update social media again, and connect with clients.

4pm Dinner.

5pm More work for clients, blogging and marketing my business, administrative tasks for my business, and / or social networking.

7:30pm Break to watch a movie or TV show on Netflix, or to read a book.

10:30pm Bed time.

As you can see from the above, business-related tasks generally took up about eight or nine hours of my day. This was a typical day for me for my first year of being a full-time freelancer, and I did this at least five days of the week, if not all seven days. Even if I chose not to work eight or nine hours on the weekend, I'd still generally put in at least four or five hours on weekend days.

This is what a typical day looked like for me after about a year of full-time freelancing:

7am Wake up, clean up and get ready for the day.

7:30am Eat breakfast at my computer while checking emails and updating social media.

8am Do some work on my blog and for clients.

9:30am Eat a snack and wash dishes while listening to a podcast.

10am Work on a product (such as writing this book!).

11:45am Walk to the gym and do a group fitness class.

12:45pm Walk home, shower, and eat lunch while listening to another podcast (sometimes I might read a book while listening to music instead, or I might do a little bit of cleaning after finishing lunch).

2pm Continue working on my blog or for clients.

4pm Walk to meet my partner on his way home from work.

5pm Arrive home, make and eat dinner, and spend some time with each other.

6:30pm Finish up with my work.

7:30pm Watch Netflix or read a book.

9pm Bedtime.

Once or twice a week, I'll go for coffee with a freelancing friend or to have a work meeting in mid-morning. You can see that now I do much less marketing and searching for work—I spend the majority of my time actually *doing* work, because I have several long-term clients and because the work often comes to me now instead of me seeking it out.

APPENDIX V: SAMPLE INVOICE

YOUR NAME

YOUR JOB TITLE

Telephone: YOUR PHONE NUMBER

Email: YOUR EMAIL ADDRESS

Website: YOUR WEBSITE

GST: YOUR BUSINESS NUMBER

INVOICE

Client: CLIENT NAME

Project: PROJECT NAME

Rate: YOUR AGREED-UPON RATE

Date Issued: TODAY'S DATE

Payment Due: DUE DATE (I recommend choosing 15 days from the day of invoicing.)

Item	Quantity	Amount
ITEM NAME	(e.g. one month / one article)	$____.__
GST	% AMOUNT	$____.__
TOTAL		$____.__

Payable via cheque. Please mail to:

YOUR MAILING ADDRESS

APPENDIX VI: SAMPLE INCOME & EXPENSES TEMPLATE (FOR BUDGETING)

This template is very basic, but it's effective for budgeting purposes! I use mine to track household and business expenses—absolutely everything I spend my money on, and every penny that comes in, gets included in these spreadsheets. It makes it much easier when tax time comes around to send it along to the accountant.

What you need to do is open an Excel spreadsheet. The first sheet should include the following columns:

Month	Income	Expense	Result	GST Owed
January 2016				
February 2016				
March 2016				
April 2016				
May 2016				
June 2016				
July 2016				
August 2016				
September 2016				
October 2016				
November 2016				
December 2016				
TOTAL	=SUM(B2:B13)	=SUM(C2:C13)	=SUM(B14-C14)	=SUM(E2:E13)

The next 24 sheets should include the following sheets, alternating between income and expenses for each month (two sheets per month, with one sheet for the income and one sheet for the expenses):

Date	Business	Product / Service	Payment Type	Amount	Notes
TOTAL				=SUM(E2:E__)	

I recommend using different colored highlighters for business expenses, bills, etc. so you can find them more easily come tax season.

APPENDIX VII: SAMPLE CONTRACT TEMPLATE

Business name: [Your business name—not needed if your business name is your own name]

Freelancer: {Your name}

Client: {Your client's name—I recommend including both the name of the person who hired you and the name of the business}

Project: {Title of the project}

This contract recognizes that {your name} has been contracted in a freelance capacity by {client's name} to complete {project name}.

The project will include the following components: {scope of the project—I recommend outlining this in list form to make it easier to read. You don't have to go into great detail, but have the rough parameters set up}.

{Your name} will complete the project by {deadline}, barring any unforeseen complications, at which point {your name} will advise {client name} as to the issues as soon as possible.

{Client's name} will pay {your name} the agreed-upon fee of {amount} no later than {date—I recommend 15 days after the project due date. You can also specify here that the fee will be paid half upon signing the contract and the other half upon submitting the completed project if it is for an especially large sum}.

{Your signature}	{Client's signature}
{Your name}	{Client's name}
{Date}	{Date}

APPENDIX VIII: SAMPLE DAILY MAINTENANCE CHECKLIST TEMPLATE

Create your own checklist with your everyday or weekly tasks, then print it out and place it in a clear plastic sheet protector. Use a dry-erase marker to check off the boxes in the first column as you complete them, and wipe it clean at the end of each workday!

The below is a sample of what I used when I was doing a lot of social media work for clients (and starting my own professional blog). Adjust as needed when you create your own to make sure it fits with your schedule and workload.

Daily Social Media Maintenance

MY BLOG

	Write new blog post
	Leave comments on 5 other blogs
	Update plugins, About page etc. as needed
	Link-up post to linky parties

MY FACEBOOK & TWITTER PAGES

	Share today's post on my Facebook page
	Re-share a relevant post from someone else on Facebook
	Participate in FB groups
	Tweet today's post
	ReTweet a relevant post from some-one else

	Share an archived post from my blog on Twitter

CLIENT A

	Write blog post (one / week) and submit
	Submit invoice (at the end of each month)

CLIENT B

	Tweet a recent blog post
	ReTweet someone else
	Write new blog post (once each week)
	Post blog article on Facebook (once each week)

CLIENT C

	Tweet with link to website / Facebook / newsletter
	ReTweet someone else
	Participate in a live Twitter chat (once each week)
	Tweet a photo / quote / news item
	Interact with 3 other posts on Facebook
	Post a news item resource on Facebook
	Share a photo / quote / event on FB
	Create and schedule newsletter (once each month)

ACKNOWLEDGEMENTS

A heartfelt thank you to...

Dan, my favorite freelancer buddy, who spent many mornings chatting over coffee with me about our experiences working from home;

Lianne, who asked all the best questions about freelancing and who was the first to read this book in its entirety and provide excellent feedback;

And Justin, for your unwavering support—you never questioned my abilities or drive when I decided to start my own business.